Easy Four-Patch Quilting™

Edited by
Jeanne Stauffer and Sandra L. Hatch

HOUSE of
WHITE
BIRCHES

Editors: Sandra L. Hatch, Jeanne Stauffer
Associate Editor: Barb Sprunger
Copy Editors: Cathy Reef, Mary Jo Kurten

Photography: Tammy Christian, Nancy Sharp
Photography Assistants: Linda Quinlan, Arlou Wittwer

Creative Coordinator: Shaun Venish
Production Artist: Brenda Gallmeyer
Traffic Coordinator: Sandra Beres
Technical Artist: Connie Rand
Production Assistants: Shirley Blalock, Carol Dailey, Cheryl Lynch
Book Design: Klaus Rothe
Cover Design: Sandy Bauman

Publishers: Carl H. Muselman, Arthur K. Muselman
Chief Executive Officer: John Robinson
Marketing Director: Scott Moss
Editorial Director: Vivian Rothe
Production Director: George Hague

Printed in the United States of America
First Printing: 1998
Library of Congress Number: 98-73376
ISBN: 1-882138-40-6

Every effort has been made to ensure the accuracy and completeness of the instructions in this book. However, we cannot be responsible for human error, for the results when using materials other than those specified in the instructions or for variations in individual work.

Front cover: Starry Night, page 121.

Simple Four-Patch

When you think of a Four-Patch design you probably visualize four squares sewn together. The basic design is that simple, but it can become more complicated as the four squares are each divided into segments or shapes. A Four-Patch design could have 80 pieces, depending on how many times one quarter of the block is divided.

Although no one knows exactly how the Four-Patch design was discovered or by whom, historians guess that most designs were created by folding paper. Further folding each quarter of the paper yields many more designs. Other patterns may have developed the same way.

Simple Four-Patch patterns can be made using quick cutting and piecing methods to save time and energy. Early quiltmakers may not have used these methods because they used mostly scraps to create their quilts. Although some of the projects in this book use scraps, quick methods can be used for most of them.

As you turn the pages of this book you might try to isolate the Four-Patch unit in each project. For some projects, this may seem impossible, but keep looking and finally you will find it.

Whether you want to make garments, household items, quilts, holiday projects or decorator wall quilts, there is something for everyone in this book. The variety of projects as well as methods and skill levels will entice beginners and experienced quilters alike. If you prefer making projects today and using them tomorrow or you're a traditionalist who works months to perfect a family heirloom there is something here for you.

Settle down for a few hours to enjoy looking through the pages. Have a pencil and paper handy to jot down the projects you might like to try right away. Plan ahead to make gifts for those very special people in your life. Organize and prioritize; make a shopping list. Before you know it, you will be on your way to completing your first Four-Patch project—just one of many.

EASY FOUR-PATCH QUILTING

Four-Patch quilts can be simple or complex. You'll find projects to complete in just a few hours and projects that will take several months. Four-Patch quilting is for everyone!

FOUR-PATCH
FUN

Get ready for some fun quilting. Start with a basic Four-Patch design and turn it into a man's tie and vest, a tissue box cover in striking Amish colors, an elegant clutch purse, a bright and cheery valance for a child's room, country patched-hearts place mats and coasters, a snazzy denim shirt design and much more. You'll enjoy using this traditional design to create these fun and fabulous projects.

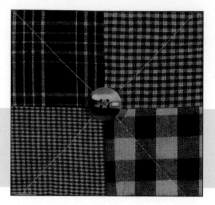

By Ann Boyce

Four-Patch Vest, Tie & Button Jumper

Men wear vests under suit jackets or with shirts. Make the vest shown in neutral colors and add this appliqué tie for a neat fashion statement.

Four-Patch Vest

BEGINNER SKILL

SPECIFICATIONS

Vest Size: Size varies

Block Size: 6" x 9"

Number of Blocks: 18

MATERIALS

☐ Purchased men's vest pattern

☐ 1/4 yard each 4 different beige plaids (58" wide)

☐ Yardage listed on pattern for vest back and lining

☐ 2 pieces cotton batting 22" x 40"

☐ 1 spool tan all-purpose thread

☐ Backing 45" x 45"

☐ 4 (7/8") mottled brown buttons

INSTRUCTIONS

STEP 1. Cut two strips from each beige plaid 3 1/2" by fabric width. Cut each strip into 5" segments. You will need 18 rectangles of each plaid.

STEP 2. Join one 3 1/2" x 5" rectangle of each fabric to make a Four-Patch block as shown in Figure 1; press. Repeat for 18 blocks.

STEP 3. Join blocks as shown in Figure 2 to make two pieced sec-

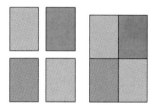

Figure 1
Join 3 1/2" x 5" rectangles
to make 1 block.

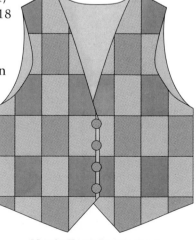

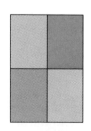

Four-Patch
6" x 9" Block

Men's Four-Patch Vest
Placement Diagram
Size Varies

tions, reversing one to make left and right vest fronts. Press seams in one direction.

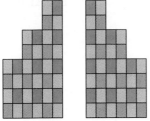

Figure 2
Join blocks to make 2 pieced sections.

STEP 4. Place one piece batting under each pieced section. Machine-quilt through centers of rectangles as shown in Figure 3.

Figure 3
Machine-quilt as shown.

STEP 5. Cut out vest fronts using purchased vest pattern.

STEP 6. Finish vest as directed in pattern instructions to finish, adding buttons and buttonholes on vest front.

Four-Patch Tie

BEGINNER SKILL

SPECIFICATIONS

Tie Size: Size varies

Block Size: 2" x 2", 2 1/2" x 2 1/2" and 3" x 3"

Number of Blocks: 1 of each size

MATERIALS

☐ Purchased necktie or tie pattern

☐ Tie fabric and lining as listed on pattern

☐ 3 squares each of 4 different plaids in the following sizes: 2" x 2", 1 3/4" x 1 3/4" and 1 1/2" x 1 1/2"

☐ 1 spool coordinating all-purpose thread

☐ Basic sewing supplies and tools

INSTRUCTIONS

STEP 1. Join four same-size plaid squares to make a Four-Patch block as shown in Figure 1. Repeat to make three different size Four-Patch blocks.

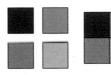

Figure 1
Join 4 same-size squares to make a Four-Patch block.

STEP 2. Turn under edges of each block 1/4"; press.

STEP 3. If using commercial pattern to make tie, construct tie front according to pattern instructions.

STEP 4. Position the three Four-Patch squares on the bottom front of tie, starting at the bottom point with the largest square about 1 3/8" from sides of point as shown in Figure 2; pin in place. Place the next largest size square tip to tip with the pinned square; repeat with smallest square. *Note: If using a purchased tie, unfold tie end to make flat before pinning and stitching. Refold when stitching is complete.*

STEP 5. Using a machine blind stitch, appliqué squares in place.

STEP 6. Complete tie construction following commercial tie pattern instructions.

Four-Patch Tie
Placement Diagram
Size Varies

Four-Patch
2" x 2", 2 1/2" x 2 1/2" & 3" x 3" Blocks

Figure 2
Place 3" Four-Patch block 1 3/8" from tip of tie.

Finished edge
1/4" is turned under
Raw edge
1/2"
1/4"
5/8"
Seam Allowance

Button Jumper

SPECIFICATIONS

Jumper Size: Size varies

Block Size: 5" x 5"

Number of Blocks: 15

MATERIALS

- ☐ Purchased jumper pattern with bodice top
- ☐ Fabrics as listed on pattern for jumper skirt and bodice lining plus 1/4 yard (beige check)
- ☐ 1/4 yard each 4 different tan-and-black checks or plaids
- ☐ Batting 20" x 32"
- ☐ 1 spool coordinating all-purpose thread
- ☐ 12 (3/4") mottled beige/brown buttons
- ☐ Basic sewing supplies and tools

INSTRUCTIONS

STEP 1. Cut 15 squares of each of the four different tan-and-black checks or plaids 3" x 3".

STEP 2. Join one square of each fabric to make a Four-Patch block

as shown in Figure 1; repeat for 15 identical blocks.

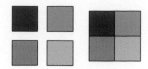

Figure 1
Join 4 squares to make a Four-Patch block.

STEP 3. Cut one 20" x 32" rectangle and 12 sashing strips 1 1/2" x 5 1/2" and three sashing strips 1 1/2" x 29 1/2" from beige check.

STEP 4. Join five Four-Patch blocks with three 1 1/2" x 5 1/2" sashing strips to make a row as shown in Figure 2; repeat for three rows. Join rows with 1 1/2" x 29 1/2" sashing strips, starting with a strip and ending with a block row as shown in Figure 3; press seams toward strips.

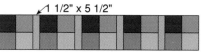

1 1/2" x 5 1/2"

Figure 2
Join sashing strips with blocks as shown.

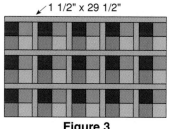

1 1/2" x 29 1/2"

Figure 3
Join 3 block rows with 3 sashing strips as shown.

STEP 5. Place the 20" x 32" beige check piece wrong side up on flat surface; place batting on top. Place pieced patchwork section right side up on batting. Pin or baste layers together.

STEP 6. Machine-quilt through all layers as shown in Figure 4. Place jumper front piece on quilted patchwork section; cut out as shown in Figure 5.

STEP 7. Sew a button in the center of each Four-Patch block and at corners of blocks on sashing strips.

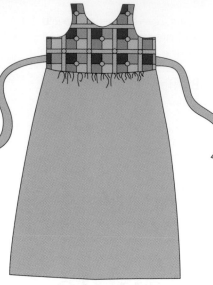

Button Jumper
Placement Diagram
Size Varies

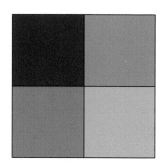

Four-Patch
5" x 5" Block

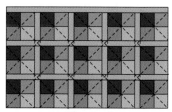

Figure 4
Machine-quilt as shown.

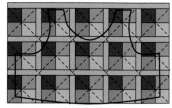

Figure 5
Place jumper pattern on patchwork section; cut out.

STEP 8. Construct jumper using purchased pattern instructions to finish. ■

By Beth Wheeler

Double Four-Patch Vest

Can you pick out the Four-Patch block in this vest? Probably not because the fabrics and design make it look complicated. It is quick to stitch, so get the materials together and get started.

PROJECT NOTE
For a random, scrappy look, choose a medium-value print as the main fabric. For a bold, controlled look, choose the lightest or darkest-value print for the main fabric.

INSTRUCTIONS
STEP 1. Cut four strips 1 1/2" by fabric width floral print. Cut one strip each four remaining fabrics 1 1/2" by fabric width.

STEP 2. Sew one strip floral print together with each of the remaining strips along length of strips. Press seams to one side.

STEP 3. Cut 1 1/2" segments from each strip set as shown in Figure 1. You will need 26 segments from each set.

STEP 4. Join two different 1 1/2" segments to make a Four-Patch unit as shown in Figure 2; press. Repeat for 52 Four-Patch units.

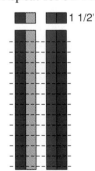

Figure 1
Cut 1 1/2" segments
from stitched strip.

1 1/2"

Figure 2
Join 2 segments to
make a Four-Patch unit.

INTERMEDIATE SKILL

SPECIFICATIONS
Vest Size: Size varies

Block Size: 2" x 2"

Number of Blocks: 106

MATERIALS
- Purchased vest pattern
- 1/4 yard two different black-and-red prints, red stripe and red plaid
- 1/2 yard floral print plus yardage listed on pattern for vest backing and lining
- 1 1/2 yards lightweight fusible interfacing
- Batting 32" x 40"
- 4 1/2 yards self-made or purchased binding
- Coordinating all-purpose thread
- Clear monofilament
- Basic sewing supplies and tools, rotary cutter, ruler, cutting mat and chalk pencil

Four-Patch
2" x 2" Block

Striped Block
2" x 2"

Double Four-Patch Vest
Placement Diagram
Size Varies

STEP 5. Cut one strip each across fabric width in the following strip sizes: 1", 1 1/4", 1 3/8" and 1 1/2". Cut one more strip each 1" by fabric width red stripe and one 1 1/4" by fabric width floral print.

STEP 6. Sew strips together along long edges, alternating widths (narrow, wide, narrow, etc.) and fabrics. Press seams in one direction.

STEP 7. Bond the fusible interfacing to the wrong side of the stitched strip set. Cut a 2 1/2" x 2 1/2" square from strips as shown in Figure 3; repeat for 54 Striped blocks.

Figure 3
Cut 2 1/2" squares from stitched strip set as shown.

STEP 8. Join Four-Patch and Striped blocks into 10 right-side rows as shown in Figure 4. *Note: Carefully position Striped blocks to place the stripes horizontally when sewn on the vest.*

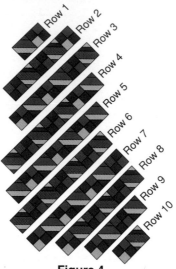

Figure 4
Join Four-Patch and Striped blocks into 10 right-side rows.

STEP 9. Join Four-Patch and Striped blocks into 10 left-side rows as shown in Figure 5. *Note: Carefully position Striped blocks to place the stripes vertically when sewn on the vest.*

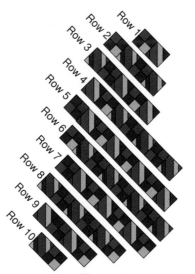

Figure 5
Join Four-Patch and Striped blocks into 10 left-side rows.

STEP 10. Using purchased vest pattern, cut two fronts from batting 1" larger all around than pattern.

STEP 11. Mark a line on both batting pieces at a 45-degree angle as shown in Figure 6. Place row 6 blocks on the left front along marked line as shown in Figure 7. Place row 5 right sides together with row 6 as shown in Figure 8; stitch. Press stitched sections flat; continue sewing rows to batting until batting is covered. Repeat for right side of vest. *Note: If there are areas of batting left uncovered, use cut-off sections after trimming to fill spaces.*

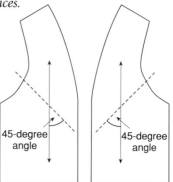

Figure 6
Mark a line on each batting piece at a 45-degree angle as shown.

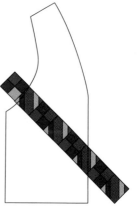

Figure 7
Place stitched row 6 along marked line for left front.

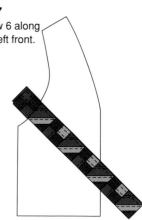

Figure 8
Place row 5 right sides together with row 6; stitch.

STEP 12. When batting has been covered, place vest pattern pieces on top; cut to shape as shown in Figure 9.

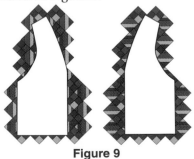

Figure 9
Place vest pattern on covered batting pieces.

STEP 13. Cut two fronts and two backs from floral print.

STEP 14. Stitch two fronts and one back piece together along shoulder and side seams for lining using a 5/8" seam allowance; press seams open.

STEP 15. Stitch pieced fronts and remaining back piece together along shoulder and side seams using a 5/8" seam allowance; press seams open. Reduce bulk in seams by cutting batting away where possible.

STEP 16. Pin vest shell and lin-

ing with wrong sides together, matching shoulder seams and corners. Stitch around vest armholes and outside edges using a 3/4" seam allowance; trim seam allowance to 1/4".

STEP 17. Stitch in the ditch of side seams using monofilament in the top of the machine and all-purpose thread in the bobbin.

STEP 18. Bind outside edges and armholes with self-made or purchased binding to finish. ■

By Norma Storm

Patched Hearts Coasters & Place Mats

Hearts pieced from pastel scrap-pieced Four-Patch units are used to create these pretty table accessories.

Place Mats

INTERMEDIATE SKILL

SPECIFICATIONS
Place Mat Size: 14 1/2" x 18"

Number of Place Mats: 2

MATERIALS
☐ 1 yard muslin for background

☐ Scraps pink, blue, green, yellow, peach and lavender prints and solids for hearts

☐ 2 pieces fleece or low-loft batting 16" x 20"

☐ All-purpose thread to match scrap fabrics

☐ Basic sewing supplies and tools, rotary cutter, ruler, cutting mat and washable pencil

INSTRUCTIONS
STEP 1. Cut four pieces muslin 18 1/2" x 15"; set aside two pieces for backing.

STEP 2. Mark a line 1/2" from edge all around each muslin background piece using washable pencil. Mark a 3 1/2"-square grid inside drawn line as shown in Figure 1 to make five squares across and four squares down, leaving one 7" x 7" area open.

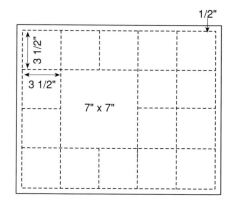

Figure 1
Mark a 3 1/2"-square grid
inside marked 1/2" lines.

STEP 3. To make a small Four-Patch Heart, cut four 2 1/4" x 2 1/4" squares from assorted scraps. Join squares to make a Four-Patch unit; press seams open. Repeat for 32 units.

STEP 4. Prepare template for small heart shape. Trace heart shape on the right side of Four-Patch units, matching lines on heart to seams on Four-Patch unit, in either square or diagonal directions as shown in Figure 2. Cut out heart shapes, adding a 1/4" seam allowance all around when cutting, using diagonal lines for 16 and square lines for 16.

Figure 2
Place heart shapes on
Four-Patch units as shown.

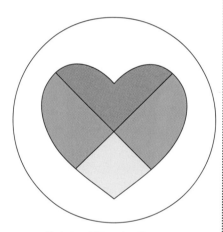

Patched Hearts Coaster
Placement Diagram
3 5/8" Diameter

STEP 5. Center a small heart in one drawn square on marked muslin background; pin to hold in place. Turn under seam allowance all around; hand-appliqué heart to background. Repeat for 16 hearts on each background referring to the Placement Diagram for positioning of small hearts.

STEP 6. To make a large heart, cut four squares 3 1/2" x 3 1/2" from assorted scraps. Join squares to make a Four-Patch unit; repeat for two units. Complete large heart as for small heart in Step 4.

STEP 7. Center large heart on muslin background referring to the Placement Diagram for positioning. Hand-appliqué heart to background; repeat for second place mat.

STEP 8. Center an appliquéd top right side up on a piece of fleece or batting. Place one of the remaining muslin rectangles right sides together with appliquéd top. Pin layers together; repeat for second place mat.

STEP 9. Stitch all around, leaving a 6" opening on one edge. Clip corners; trim edges. Turn right side out through opening; press. Hand-stitch opening closed.

STEP 10. Using decorative stitches and different color threads to match scraps, stitch on the

drawn lines on muslin background. Pull thread ends to the backside, tie securely and trim.

Patched Hearts Coasters

INTERMEDIATE SKILL

SPECIFICATIONS

Coaster Size: 3 5/8" diameter

Number of Coasters: 2

MATERIALS

☐ 8 squares 2 1/4" x 2 1/4" assorted pastel fabrics

☐ 9" square muslin for background and backing

☐ 9" square fusible interfacing

☐ All-purpose thread to match scrap fabrics

☐ Basic sewing supplies and tools, rotary cutter, ruler, cutting mat and washable pencil

INSTRUCTIONS

STEP 1. Prepare template for coaster circle. Cut as directed.

STEP 2. Prepare two Four-Patch units and two small hearts as in Steps 3 and 4 for Place Mats.

STEP 3. Bond fusible interfacing to wrong side of four muslin circles, centering interfacing inside seam allowance.

STEP 4. Fold one interfaced circle in half; cut a small slit at center fold. Unfold; make slit about 1" wide. Layer right sides together with another muslin circle; stitch all around. Clip curves; turn right side out through slit and press. Repeat for two circles.

STEP 5. Center a pieced heart over slit in circle. Hand-stitch in place as for Place Mat Step 5; repeat.

STEP 6. Using thread to match scraps and a decorative machine stitch, sew around outside edges of each coaster to finish. ■

Patched Hearts Place Mat
Placement Diagram
14 1/2" x 18"

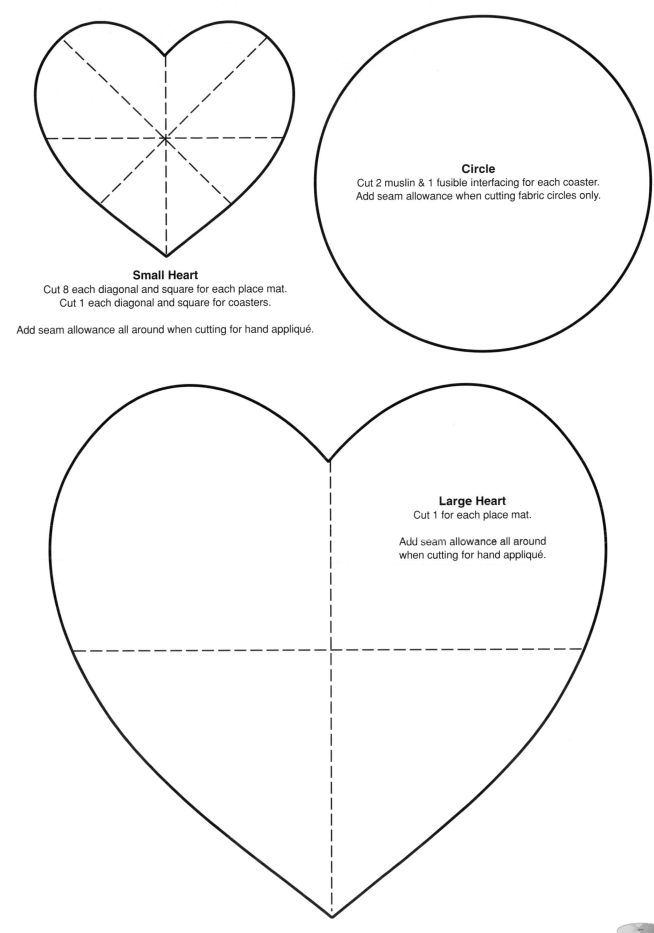

Small Heart
Cut 8 each diagonal and square for each place mat.
Cut 1 each diagonal and square for coasters.

Add seam allowance all around when cutting for hand appliqué.

Circle
Cut 2 muslin & 1 fusible interfacing for each coaster.
Add seam allowance when cutting fabric circles only.

Large Heart
Cut 1 for each place mat.

Add seam allowance all around when cutting for hand appliqué.

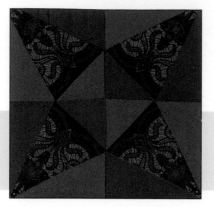

By Charlyne Stewart

Quilted Treasure Boxes

Make these pretty quilted boxes to hold a myriad of treasures. Fill them with sewing supplies, jewelry, photos or any important thing that needs a safe niche.

Large Box

INTERMEDIATE SKILL

SPECIFICATIONS

Box Size: 10" x 10" x 4"

Block Size: 10" x 10"

Number of Blocks: 1

MATERIALS

- □ 1/4 yard each light and dark purple solid
- □ 1 yard blue/purple print
- □ 2/3 yard thin fleece
- □ 1 piece thin batting 11" x 11"
- □ All-purpose thread to match fabrics
- □ 1 spool matching quilting thread
- □ 1 sheet illustration board or cardboard 20" x 20"
- □ Basic tools, craft knife, plus special supplies

INSTRUCTIONS

STEP 1. Prepare templates using pattern pieces given.

STEP 2. Cut two 10" x 10" squares and four 4" x 10" rectangles from cardboard or illustration board. *Note: Cut by scoring lines with a craft knife and metal straight edge to start and scissors to finish on top of a self-healing mat.*

STEP 3. Using cardboard squares and rectangles as templates, mark one square and four rectangles on fold of blue/purple print adding 1/4" seam allowance as shown in Figure 1; cut out. Mark two squares and four rectangles on fold of fleece, adding 1/4" seam allowance; cut out. *Note: This step yields one 10 1/2" x 20 1/2" and four 4 1/2" x 20 1/2" pieces*

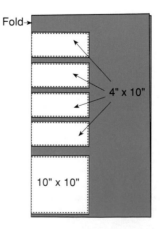

Fold →

4" x 10"

10" x 10"

Figure 1
Mark squares and rectangles on fold of print fabric; add 1/4" seam allowance.

blue/purple print, two 10 1/2" x 20 1/2" and four 4 1/2" x 20 1/2" pieces fleece.

STEP 4. Place a cardboard square between folded 10 1/2" x 20 1/2" fleece piece; stitch around all sides to enclose cardboard. Trim fleece close to stitching. Repeat with remaining square and rectangles. *Note: Set aside one fleece/cardboard for use in Step 8.*

STEP 5. Stitch around two edges of 10 1/2" x 20 1/2" print piece folded with right sides together to make a pocket; turn right side out. Slip fleece/cardboard square inside. Fold in seam allowance on open edges; whipstitch closed to finish box bottom. Repeat with 4 1/2" x 20 1/2" print pieces and fleece/cardboard rectangles to make box sides.

Figure 2
Sew A and AR to B; add C.

STEP 6. Sew A and AR to B as shown in Figure 2; repeat for four units. Add light purple C to two units and dark purple C to two units.

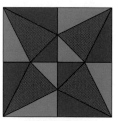

Sugar Cone
8" x 8" Block

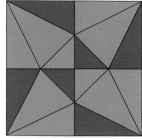

Sugar Cone
10" x 10" Block

Figure 3
Join 4 pieced units to complete 1 block.

STEP 7. Cut one 11" x 11" square blue/purple print. Sandwich with pieced block and 11" x 11" batting square. Quilt in the ditch of seams and as desired by hand or machine. Trim edge even with pieced block.

STEP 8. Cut one 10 1/2" x 10 1/2" square blue/purple print; place right sides together with quilted block. Sew around three sides; clip curves. Turn right side out. Slip remaining fleece/cardboard square inside. Fold in seam allowance on open edges; whipstitch closed to finish box top.

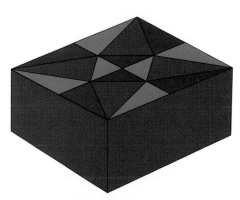

Quilted Treasure Box
Placement Diagram
8" x 8" x 3 1/2"

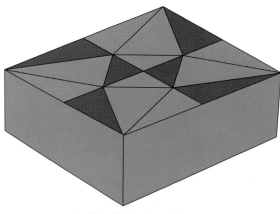

Quilted Treasure Box
Placement Diagram
10" x 10" x 4"

STEP 9. Whipstitch box sides to box bottom on outside edges and at corners to make box bottom. Whipstitch box top to one side to finish.

Small Box

INTERMEDIATE SKILL

SPECIFICATIONS
Box Size: 8" x 8" x 3 1/2"
Block Size: 8" x 8"
Number of Blocks: 1

MATERIALS
☐ 1/6 yard each teal and magenta solids
☐ 2/3 yard teal print
☐ 1/2 yard thin fleece
☐ 1 piece batting 9" x 9"
☐ All-purpose thread
☐ 1 spool quilting thread
☐ 1 sheet illustration board or cardboard 16" x 16"
☐ Basic sewing tools and supplies, metal straight edge, marking pencil, self-healing mat, craft knife and template plastic

INSTRUCTIONS
STEP 1. Follow instructions for Large Box except use A2, B2 and C2 templates and substitute appropriate fabrics, referring to Placement Diagram for color placement.

STEP 2. Substitute the following sizes for Small Box: Step 3 will yield one 8 1/2" x 16 1/2" and four 4" x 16 1/2" pieces teal print, two 8 1/2" x 16 1/2" and four 4" x 16 1/2" pieces fleece. These pieces are used in Steps 4 and 5. For Step 7, cut one 9" x 9" square teal print. For Step 8, cut one 8 1/2" x 8 1/2" square teal print.

STEP 3. Cut two 8" x 8" squares and four 8" x 3 1/2" rectangles from cardboard or illustration board.

STEP 4. Complete construction as for Large Box. ■

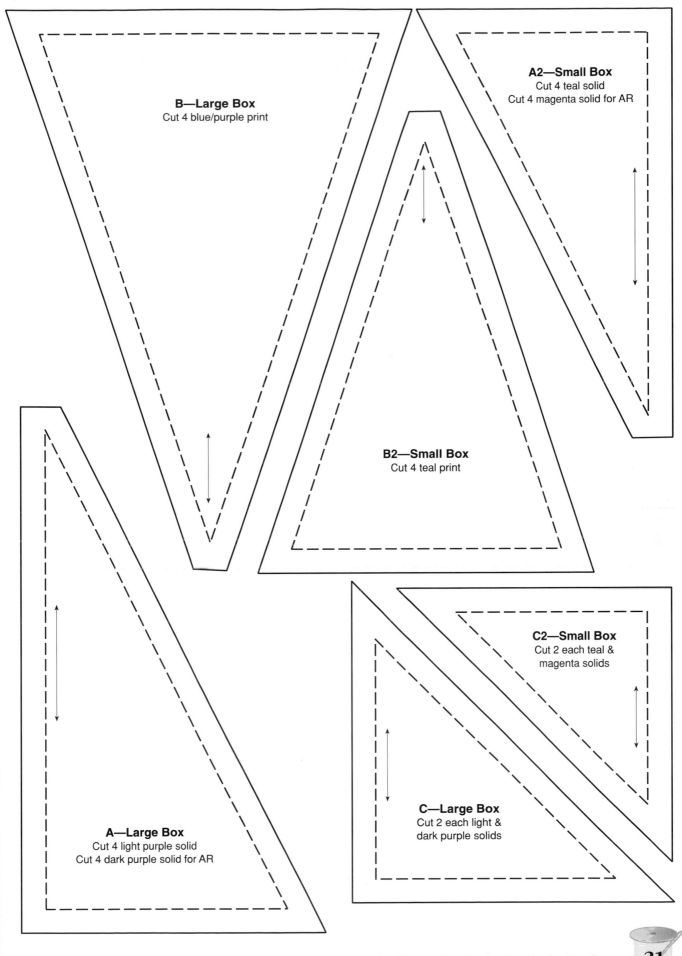

B—Large Box
Cut 4 blue/purple print

A2—Small Box
Cut 4 teal solid
Cut 4 magenta solid for AR

B2—Small Box
Cut 4 teal print

C2—Small Box
Cut 2 each teal &
magenta solids

C—Large Box
Cut 2 each light &
dark purple solids

A—Large Box
Cut 4 light purple solid
Cut 4 dark purple solid for AR

By Ruth Swasey

Rolling Four-Patch Valance

Brighten up a bedroom or bath with this colorful window treatment based on the Four-Patch design.

BEGINNER SKILL

SPECIFICATIONS
Valance Size: 8 1/2" x 60"

Block Size: 6" x 6"

Number of Blocks: 10

MATERIALS
☐ 1/4 yard each 4 different blue prints

☐ 1/4 yard yellow check

☐ 1/2 yard muslin

☐ 1/2 yard yellow print

☐ Coordinating all-purpose thread

☐ 11 (7/8") buttons

☐ Basic sewing supplies and tools

INSTRUCTIONS
STEP 1. Cut two strips each 2 7/8" by fabric width yellow print and yellow check. Join one strip of each fabric along length; press seams in one direction. Repeat with remaining two strips.

STEP 2. Cut each pieced strip into 2 7/8" segments; you will need 20 segments. Join two segments as shown in Figure 1 to make a Four-Patch unit; repeat for 10 units.

Figure 1
Join 2 segments to make
a Four-Patch unit.

STEP 3. Prepare a template for piece A using pattern piece given. Cut as directed on the piece.

STEP 4. Sew an A piece to each side of a Four-Patch unit to complete one block as shown in Figure 2; repeat for 10 blocks.

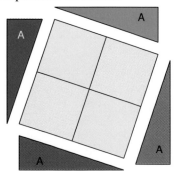

Figure 2
Sew A to each side of a Four-Patch unit.

MAKE IT
QUICK!
24 HOURS
OR LESS!

STEP 5. Join the blocks in a row tilting all Four-Patch units in the same direction referring to the Placement Diagram; press seams in one direction.

STEP 6. Cut two strips yellow print 3" by fabric width. Sew strips together on one short end; press seam open. Cut strip 60 1/2" long. Sew to top edge of pieced-block strip, referring to the Placement Diagram for positioning; press seam toward strip.

STEP 7. Prepare a template for tab piece using pattern piece given. Cut as directed on the piece.

STEP 8. Place two tabs right sides together; sew around sides and pointed end, leaving square end open as shown in Figure 3. Turn right side out; press. Repeat for 11 tabs.

STEP 9. Pin tabs to pieced valance front, placing one tab at each end and evenly spacing remaining tabs across top edge as shown in Figure 4; machine-baste tabs in place.

Rolling Four-Patch
6" x 6" Block

Figure 3
Stitch tab pieces together as shown.

Figure 4
Pin tab pieces across top edge as shown.

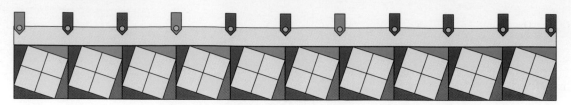

Rolling Four-Patch Valance
Placement Diagram
8 1/2" x 60"

STEP 10. Piece muslin to make a 9" x 60 1/2" backing. Lay right sides together with pieced front; sew around all sides leaving a 6" opening on one end. Turn right side out through opening. Press; hand-stitch opening closed. Topstitch close to top edge.

STEP 11. Fold tab pieces at fold line marked on template. Pin tab points in place on valance front. Hand-stitch a button on each tab to finish. ■

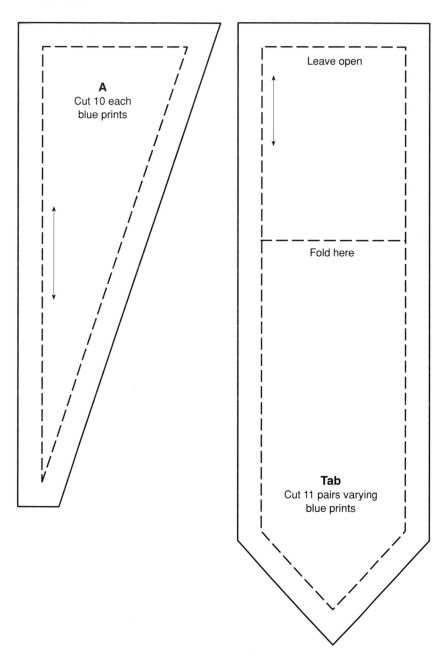

A
Cut 10 each
blue prints

Leave open

Fold here

Tab
Cut 11 pairs varying
blue prints

By Michele Crawford

Patriotic Denim Shirt

Denim shirts have moved up in the world of fashion.
Decorated shirts are expensive at retail stores but you can
make your own with this simple Four-Patch Star design.

PROJECT NOTE
A size 18 denim shirt was used to create the
sample. Adjust the number of blocks needed for
other shirt sizes.

INSTRUCTIONS
STEP 1. Prewash shirt; press.

STEP 2. Topstitch rickrack around collar,
cuffs and down both sides of front placket on
the denim shirt.

STEP 3. Cut 14 squares each navy solid and
white print 2 3/8" x 2 3/8". Cut each square in
half to make 28 triangles of each color.

STEP 4. Sew a navy solid triangle to a white
print triangle to make a triangle/square; press
seams toward navy solid. Repeat for 28 trian-
gle/square units.

STEP 5. Join four triangle/squares as shown
in Figure 1 to make a block; press. Repeat for
seven blocks.

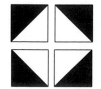

Figure 1
Join 4 triangle/squares as
shown to make a block.

STEP 6. Cut eight strips 1 1/2" x 3 1/2" and
two strips 1 1/2" x 29 1/2" patriotic print.

BEGINNER SKILL

SPECIFICATIONS
Shirt Size: Size Varies

Block Size: 3" x 3"

Number of Blocks: 7

MATERIALS
☐ Purchased long-sleeve
   denim shirt

☐ 1/8 yard navy solid

☐ 1/8 yard white print

☐ 1/6 yard patriotic print

☐ 1 strip gold print 2 1/2" x 19"

☐ 1 strip cranberry plaid
   4 1/2" x 17"

☐ 1 spool each white, navy
   denim blue, gold and cranberry all-purpose thread

☐ 1/4 yard fusible transfer web

☐ 1/8 yard tear-off fabric
   stabilizer

☐ 1 package off-white
   baby rickrack

☐ Basic sewing supplies and
   tools, rotary cutter, ruler
   and cutting mat

MAKE IT
QUICK!
24 HOURS
OR LESS!

Patriotic Denim Shirt
Placement Diagram
Size Varies

STEP 8. Sew a 1 1/2" x 29 1/2" strip to each long side of the pieced row as shown in Figure 3; press seams toward strip. Press unfinished long edges of strip under 1/4".

STEP 9. Center the pieced block strip on the right shirt front 1 1/2" from the outside of the placket. Turn the edges of the strip under to fit along smoothly at the shoulder seam and the shirt hem. Pin the strip to the shirt. Hand-stitch the strip in place.

STEP 10. Bond the gold print and cranberry plaid fabric pieces to the fusible transfer web. Trace seven small stars on the fused gold print and four small stars and one large star on the fused cranberry plaid using patterns given. Cut out shapes along traced lines; peel off paper backing.

STEP 11. Center the large cranberry plaid star on the shirt pocket, a gold star on the large cranberry star and three gold stars above pocket; fuse in place.

STEP 12. Beginning with a cranberry star on the top pieced square, alternate stars on each square; fuse in place.

STEP 13. Place a piece of fabric stabilizer behind each star above pocket. Machine-appliqué all stars in place using matching threads. Remove stabilizer from behind stars above pocket to finish. ■

STEP 7. Join the seven blocks with eight 1 1/2" x 3 1/2" strips beginning and ending with a strip to make a block row as shown in Figure 2; press seams toward strips.

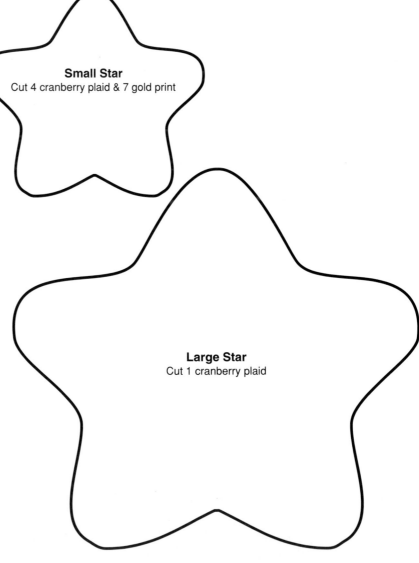

Small Star
Cut 4 cranberry plaid & 7 gold print

Large Star
Cut 1 cranberry plaid

1 1/2" x 3 1/2"

1 1/2" x 29 1/2"

Figure 2
Join 7 blocks with 8 strips as shown.

Figure 3
Sew a 1 1/2" x 29 1/2" strip to each long side of the pieced row.

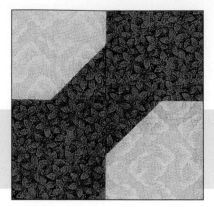

By Michele Crawford

Bow Tie Kitchen Set

Traditional Bow Tie blocks work together to coordinate a casserole-making ensemble.

BEGINNER SKILL

SPECIFICATIONS
Apron Size: One size fits all

Casserole Cover: 15" x 19"

Pot Holder Size: 8" x 8"

Block Size: 4" x 4"

Number of Blocks: 8 for pot holders, 12 for casserole cover and 4 for apron

MATERIALS
☐ 1/8 yard white floral print

☐ 1/6 yard each lavender, pink and green prints and blue stripe

☐ 1/4 yard white print

☐ 2 1/2 yards floral print

☐ 1/2 yard single-face quilted muslin

☐ 1 rectangle cotton batting 15 1/2" x 19 1/2"

☐ 4 squares cotton batting 8 1/2" x 8 1/2"

☐ 1 rectangle cotton batting 11 1/2" x 12 1/2"

☐ 12" of 1"-wide hook-and-loop tape

☐ 1 spool white all-purpose thread

☐ 1 spool clear monofilament

☐ Basic sewing supplies and tools

MAKING BLOCKS
STEP 1. Cut 12 squares each 1 1/2" x 1 1/2" and 2 1/2" x 2 1/2" from pink, lavender and green prints and blue stripe. Cut 48 squares 2 1/2" x 2 1/2" white print.

STEP 2. Place a 1 1/2" x 1 1/2" colored square on the corner of a 2 1/2" x 2 1/2" white print square; stitch across the diagonal of the small square as shown in Figure 1.

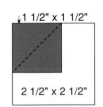

Figure 1
Place 1 1/2" x 1 1/2" colored square on 2 1/2" x 2 1/2" white square as shown. Stitch across diagonal.

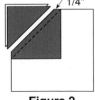

Figure 2
Trim excess away.

STEP 3. Trim excess layers as shown in Figure 2. Press the resulting colored triangle away from the white print square to complete one unit; repeat for 48 units.

STEP 4. Join units with like-colored 2 1/2" x 2 1/2" squares as shown in Figure 3 to complete one half-block unit. Join two half-block units to complete one block as shown in Figure 4; repeat for 24 blocks; press.

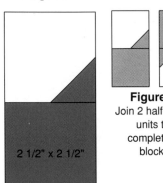

Figure 3
Sew a pieced unit to a same-color square.

Figure 4
Join 2 half-block units to complete 1 block.

Bow Tie
4" x 4" Block

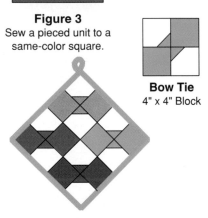

Bow Tie Pot Holder
Placement Diagram
8" x 8"

Pot Holders

STEP 1. Join one Bow Tie block of each color into a four-block unit as shown in Figure 5; press. Repeat for second unit.

STEP 2. Cut two squares quilted muslin 8 1/2" x 8 1/2". Center two batting squares on each of the quilted muslin squares; center the wrong side of a pieced four-block section on the batting; pin layers together.

STEP 3. With white all-purpose thread in the bobbin and monofilament in the top of the machine,

machine-quilt in the ditch of the seams between blocks. Topstitch around quilted piece 1/8" from edges.

STEP 4. Cut two strips 1 1/2" by fabric width floral print. Press one long edge of each strip under 1/4". Beginning at a corner, place the unfolded edge of one strip right sides together with one quilted piece; stitch all around, mitering corners. When stitching reaches the starting point, extend end about 6" and cut off.

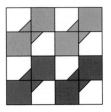

Figure 5
Join 4 Bow Tie blocks to complete a 4-block unit.

STEP 5. Fold end under 1/4"; fold strip to backside and extension in half. Stitch extension piece along edge and hand-stitch in place on the backside of pot holder to make a hanging loop. Hand-stitch binding to backside of pot holder to finish; repeat for second pot holder.

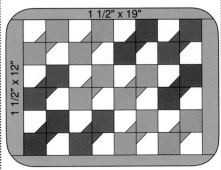

Bow Tie Casserole Cover
Placement Diagram
15" x 19"

Casserole Cover

STEP 1. Select three Bow Tie blocks of each color. Join the blocks in three rows of four blocks each, alternating colors as shown in Figure 6; join rows to complete pieced top. Press seams in one direction.

Figure 6
Join 4 blocks to make 3 rows, alternating colors as shown.

STEP 2. Cut two strips each floral print 2" x 12 1/2" and 2" x 19 1/2". Sew the 12 1/2" strips to short sides and 19 1/2" strips to top and bottom of pieced top. Press seams toward strips.

STEP 3. Prepare a pattern for casserole cover using pattern given. Cut as directed on the piece. Use pattern to cut bordered blocks to shape.

STEP 4. Center batting on the wrong side of the floral-print piece. Center the wrong side of the pieced top on the batting; pin layers together. Machine-quilt as in Step 3 for Pot Holders. Topstitch 1/8" from edge.

STEP 5. With right sides together, sew the floral print and quilted muslin shapes together along one curved edge as marked on pattern. Turn right side out; press.

STEP 6. With floral-print sides together, center the quilted top and stitched bottom pieces together; pin. Topstitch around three sides 1/8" from edge, stopping stitching on long sides 3" from short edges on one end.

STEP 7. Cut two strips floral print 1 1/2" by fabric width. Stitch strips right sides together along short ends to make one long strip for binding. Press the long edge under 1/4".

STEP 8. Place strip right sides together and raw edges even on quilted top, stitch around outside edges through both layers where previously stitched and through only the quilted layers where not previously stitched as shown in Figure 7. *Note: The binding finishes the edges of the joined top and bottom pieces on three sides, in the 3" unstitched areas on sides and around open edge of quilted section.*

STEP 9. Sew a section of hook tape on one inside edge and loop tape on other inside edge to make closure.

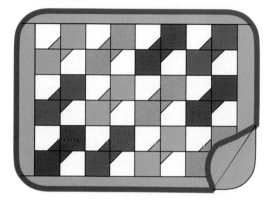

Figure 7
Bind edges as shown.

Place line on fold

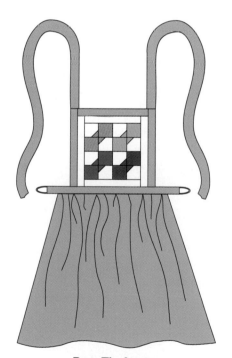

Bow Tie Apron
Placement Diagram
One Size Fits All

Apron

STEP 1. Join one Bow Tie block of each color to make a four-block unit as for Pot Holder.

STEP 2. Cut two strips each 1 1/2" x 8 1/2" and 1 1/2" x 10 1/2" white floral print. Sew an 8 1/2" strip to the top and bottom of the four-block unit. Sew a 10 1/2" strip to opposite sides; press seams toward strips.

STEP 3. Cut one strip 1 1/2" x 10 1/2" and two strips 1 1/2" x 11 1/2" floral print. Sew the 10 1/2" strip to the top of the bordered four-block unit. Sew the 11 1/2" strips to opposite sides; press seams toward strips.

STEP 4. Center the wrong side of the bordered four-block unit on the 11 1/2" x 12 1/2" rectangle batting; pin.

STEP 5. For apron ties, cut two 3 1/2" by fabric width strips floral print. Fold each strip in half right sides together along length; stitch across one short end and along length, leaving one end open. Turn right side out; press.

STEP 6. Position the outside of a strip 1/4" in from outside of the batted and bordered four-block unit as shown in Figure 8; pin in place. Repeat for second strip on opposite side. Topstitch 1/8" from edge across straps to hold.

STEP 7. Cut an 11 1/2" x 12 1/2" rectangle floral print for backing. Place right sides together with batted four-block bib front unit; pin in place. Stitch around three sides, leaving bottom edge open. Turn right side out; press.

1/4"

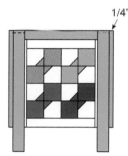

Figure 8
Stitch across straps
to hold in place.

STEP 8. Machine-quilt bib front as in Step 3 for Pot Holders. Topstitch across the open end.

STEP 9. To make waistband, cut two 2" x 22" strips floral print. Center and sew both

Continued on page 35

Casserole Cover
Cut 1 batting, 2 floral prints & 1 quilted muslin

Place line on fold

By Marian Shenk

Four-Patch Clutch Purse

The Four-Patch block used to create this elegant clutch purse is not visible unless you really search for it. This bag is simple to make and can be carried to any dressy occasion.

ADVANCED BEGINNER

SPECIFICATIONS
Purse Size: Approximately
   6" x 12"

Block Size: 12" x 12"

Number of Blocks: 1

MATERIALS
☐ 1/4 yard black silk for patchwork and gusset
☐ 1/2 yard black solid cotton for lining
☐ Scraps color silk fabrics for crazy patchwork and block
☐ 3/4 yard stiff interfacing
☐ 1 spool black all-purpose thread
☐ Fancy clasp or button
☐ Dot of hook-and-loop tape
☐ Basic sewing supplies and tools and white chalk pencil

INSTRUCTIONS
STEP 1. Prepare templates using pattern pieces given. Cut as directed on each piece.

STEP 2. Layer both pieces flap interfacing; pin. Using scraps of silk, cover interfacing layers with crazy patchwork as shown in Figure 1. Trim to conform to the shape of the interfacing flap.

Figure 1
Cover flap interfacing pieces with crazy patchwork.

STEP 3. Place black solid lining flap right sides together with crazy-patchwork flap; sew around sides and curved edge, leaving straight edge open. Clip curves and trim seams; turn right side out and press.

STEP 4. Join four B triangles as shown in Figure 2 to complete one unit; repeat for four units. Join units as shown in Figure 3; sew an A triangle to each side to complete one block; press.

STEP 5. Using pieced square as a pattern, cut one piece of stiff interfacing. Pin to wrong side of

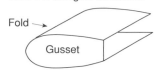

Figure 2
Join 4 B triangles as shown.

Figure 4
Set gusset into folded square.

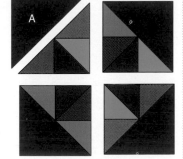

Figure 3
Join pieced units as shown;
sew A to each side.

block. Quilt in the ditch of seams as desired.

STEP 6. Cut a piece of black cotton solid and stiff interfacing 12 1/2" x 12 1/2" for lining; baste interfacing to lining square. Fold square in half.

STEP 7. Mark gusset dart on black cotton solid with chalk pencil. Baste gusset interfacing pieces to gusset pieces. Set black cotton solid gussets into sides of lining square as shown in Figure 4. Repeat with black cotton solid gusset pieces and pieced block. Sew finished flap to one straight edge of the pieced square.

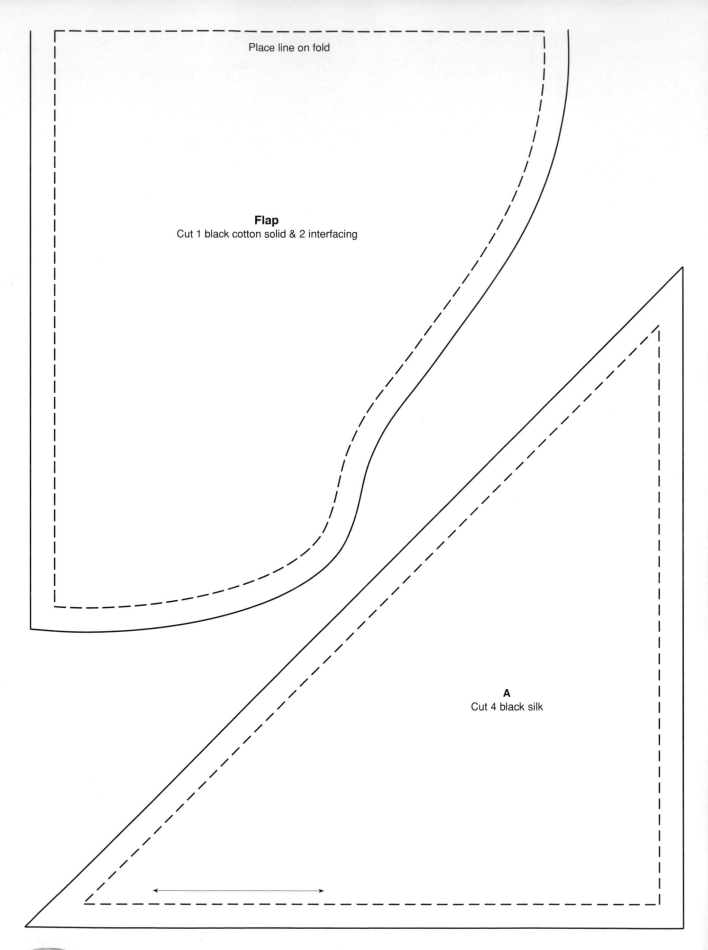

Place line on fold

Flap
Cut 1 black cotton solid & 2 interfacing

A
Cut 4 black silk

Four-Patch Clutch Purse
Placement Diagram
Approximately 6" x 12"

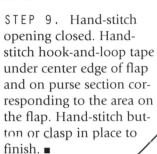

Four-Patch Pinwheel
12" x 12" Block

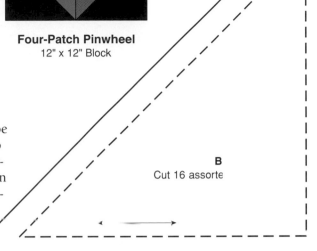

B
Cut 16 assorte

STEP 8. Place lining and finished block with flap right sides together; stitch around top edges, leaving a 4" opening. Trim seams and clip curves; turn right side out through opening. Poke out all corners. Sew gusset darts through all layers from the lining side of purse.

STEP 9. Hand-stitch opening closed. Hand-stitch hook-and-loop tape under center edge of flap and on purse section corresponding to the area on the flap. Hand-stitch button or clasp in place to finish. ■

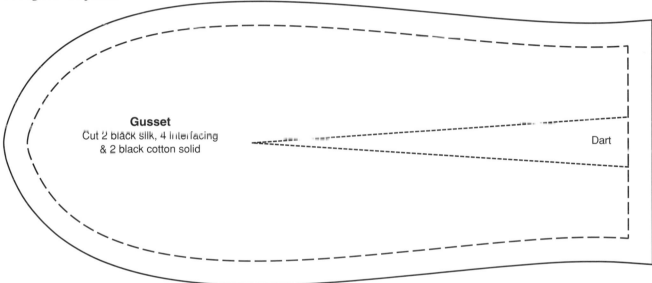

Gusset
Cut 2 black silk, 4 interfacing
& 2 black cotton solid

Dart

Bow Tie Kitchen Set

Continued from page 31

strips along the bottom edge of the apron bib, making a sandwich with the waistband, apron bib and other waistband with right sides of waistband against apron bib. Press the bottom raw edge of inside waistband under 1/4".

STEP 10. Cut a 28" by fabric width rectangle floral print for skirt. Press sides under 1/4"; turn under 1/4" again and topstitch.

Press the bottom edge under 1/4"; turn pressed edge up 1 1/2" and topstitch.

STEP 11. Sew a basting stitch across the top edge of the skirt. Gather the basting stitches so the skirt fits across the waistband 2 1/2" in from each side; topstitch.

STEP 12. Cut a 1 1/2" x 6" strip floral print. Press strip in half with wrong sides together. Unfold and press raw edges to the center press line. Refold the strip and topstitch.

STEP 13. Cut strip into two 3" lengths. Make a loop; pin to the short end of each side of waistband allowing a 1/4" seam above and below the loop; topstitch.

STEP 14. To complete waistband, flip the waistband over so that the right sides are together. Sew across the short end, turn the corner and stitch to the outside of the skirt. Turn the waistband right side out; press. Hand-stitch in place to finish. ■

By Vicki Blizzard

Let's Fly a Kite Sweatshirt

This very simple sweatshirt conveys the springtime feeling of windy days and flying kites.

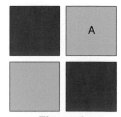

BEGINNER SKILL

SPECIFICATIONS
Sweatshirt Size: Child size

MATERIALS
☐ Child's sweatshirt in desired size

☐ Scraps of white, blue, red, yellow and green prints

☐ White and neutral color all-purpose thread

☐ 1 package white baby rickrack

☐ Fray preventive

☐ Basic sewing supplies and tools

INSTRUCTIONS
STEP 1. Prepare templates using pattern pieces given. Cut as directed on each piece.

STEP 2. Join two each red and blue print A squares to make a Four-Patch block as

Let's Fly a Kite
Placement Diagram
Child's Size

shown in Figure 1. Repeat with green and yellow prints to make a second block.

Figure 1
Join A squares to make
Four-Patch block.

STEP 3. Turn under edges of cloud pieces. Hand-appliqué in place on sweatshirt referring to the photo and Placement Diagram for positioning to finish.

STEP 4. Cut two lengths rickrack for kite tails referring to the Placement Diagram for positioning and measuring the sweatshirt for desired length. *Note: Sample lengths are 7" and 13" long.* Using white thread, hand- or machine-stitch rickrack in place.

STEP 5. Turn under edges of each Four-Patch unit 1/4" all around; pin corner of block to top of stitched rickrack. Hand-appliqué blocks in place with neutral color thread.

STEP 6. Cut four pieces rickrack each 3" long. Tie a knot in the center of each piece. Trim ends to approximately 1"; apply fray preventive to each end.

STEP 7. Hand-stitch a knotted piece of rickrack to previously stitched rickrack at the knot to make kite tails; leave ends free. ■

Continued on page 41

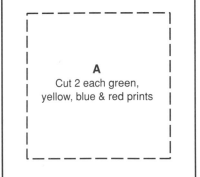

A
Cut 2 each green,
yellow, blue & red prints

By Janice McKee

Amish Weave Dresser Set

Dark jewel tone solids are used to create this matching dresser scarf and tissue box cover. If you are partial to Amish quilts, make this set to coordinate with a quilt using the same colors.

Dresser Scarf

INTERMEDIATE SKILL

SPECIFICATIONS

Dresser Scarf Size: 17" x 34"

Block Size: 6" x 6"

Number of Blocks: 8

MATERIALS

☐ 1/4 yard each red, blue, green and purple solids

☐ 3/4 yard black solid

☐ Backing 20" x 37"

☐ Batting 20" x 37"

☐ 2 1/2 yards self-made black binding

☐ 1 spool black all-purpose thread

☐ Basic sewing supplies and tools and white chalk pencil

INSTRUCTIONS

STEP 1. Cut two squares 6 1/2" x 6 1/2" black solid for

D. Prepare template; cut E triangles as directed on pattern piece.

STEP 2. For each block cut four 2 1/2" x 2 1/2" squares black, one piece each 1 1/2" x 3 1/2" for C and one piece each 1 1/2" x 2 1/2" for B from red, green, blue and purple solids; repeat for eight blocks.

STEP 3. Sew a B piece to one side of each A square; press seams toward B. Sew a C piece to the A-B units referring to Figure 1 for color placement; press seams toward C. Repeat for eight of each unit.

STEP 4. Join four pieced A-B-C units to complete one block as shown in Figure 2. Repeat for eight blocks; press.

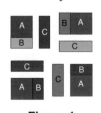

Figure 1
Sew B to A; sew
C to A-B unit.

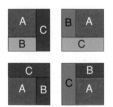

Figure 2
Join 4 A-B-C units to
complete 1 block.

STEP 5. Arrange blocks with D squares and E triangles as shown in Figure 3. Join in diagonal rows; join rows. Press seams in one direction.

MAKE IT
QUICK!
24 HOURS
OR LESS!

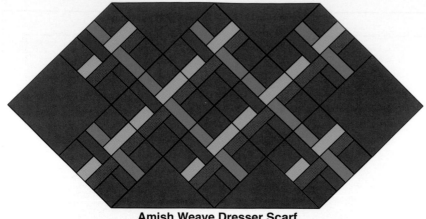

Amish Weave Dresser Scarf
Placement Diagram
17" x 34"

Amish Weave Tissue Box Cover
Placement Diagram
5 1/2" x 5 1/2" x 6"

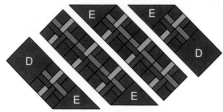

Figure 3
Arrange pieced blocks with D
squares and E triangles as shown.

STEP 6. Mark D squares and E triangles with quilting design as shown
in Figure 4 using chalk pencil.

Figure 4
Mark quilting lines on D and E
pieces as shown.

STEP 7. Quilt and finish as
directed in General Instructions.

using 1/2" seams. Join two ends to
make a box tube for box cover
sides referring to Figure 5.

Figure 5
Join 2 ends to make a box tube.

STEP 6. Turn under 1/4" on top
and bottom edges; topstitch on
outside by machine as shown in
Figure 6.

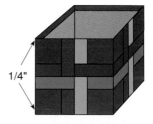

1/4"

Figure 6
Topstitch 1/4" from edges.

Tissue Box Cover

INTERMEDIATE SKILL

SPECIFICATIONS
Tissue Box Cover Size:
   5 1/2" x 5 1/2" x 6"

Block Size: 6" x 6"

Number of Blocks: 4

MATERIALS
☐ 1/4 yard black solid
☐ Scraps blue, red, green
   and purple solids

☐ 4 pieces batting 8" x 8"
☐ 4 squares backing 8" x 8"
☐ 2 pieces batting 3" x 6"
☐ 1 spool black
   all-purpose thread
☐ 4 (1/2") silver buttons
☐ 4 (8") lengths 1/8"-wide
   blue, red, green and
   purple ribbons
☐ Basic sewing supplies
   and tools

INSTRUCTIONS
STEP 1. Construct four blocks
as for Dresser Scarf Steps 2–4.

STEP 2. Place a batting square on
top of wrong side of backing
square; center pieced block on batting. Pin or baste layers together;
repeat for four blocks.

STEP 3. Hand- or machine-quilt in
the ditch of seams.

STEP 4. Trim batting and backing even with block edges; zigzag
around all edges to stabilize.

STEP 5. Join four blocks with
right sides together to make a row

STEP 7. Fold box tube at seams
adjoining two blocks; topstitch
1/4" from seams through two
blocks at once as shown in Figure
7 to form box corners.

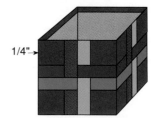

1/4"

Figure 7
Topstitch 1/4" from folded
corner with seams.

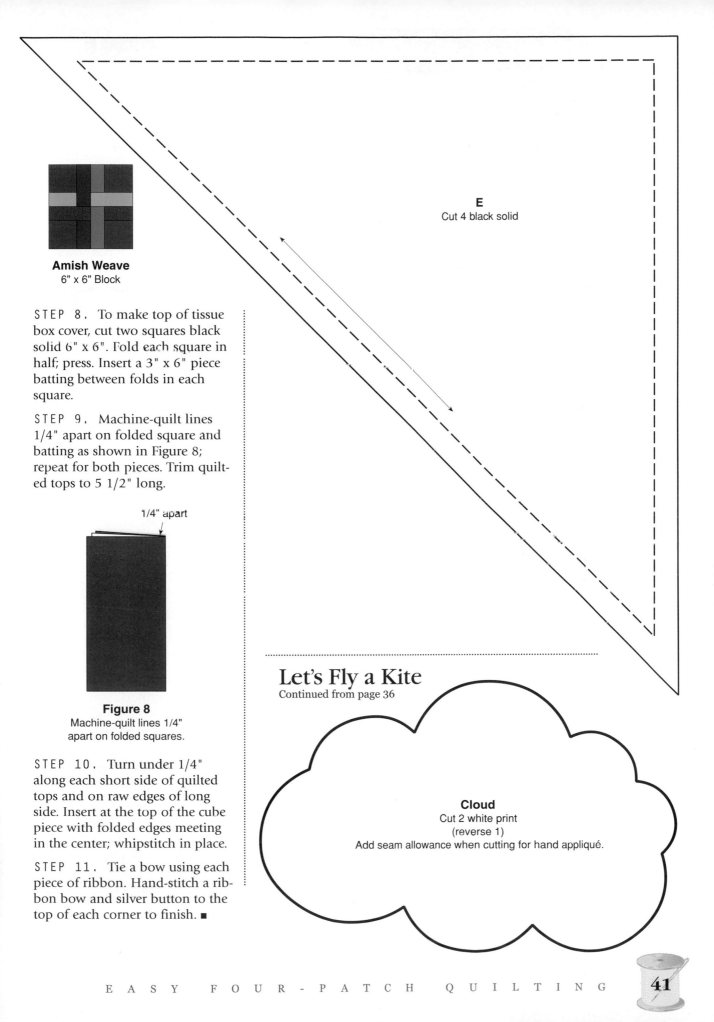

Amish Weave
6" x 6" Block

E
Cut 4 black solid

STEP 8. To make top of tissue box cover, cut two squares black solid 6" x 6". Fold each square in half; press. Insert a 3" x 6" piece batting between folds in each square.

STEP 9. Machine-quilt lines 1/4" apart on folded square and batting as shown in Figure 8; repeat for both pieces. Trim quilted tops to 5 1/2" long.

1/4" apart

Figure 8
Machine-quilt lines 1/4"
apart on folded squares.

STEP 10. Turn under 1/4" along each short side of quilted tops and on raw edges of long side. Insert at the top of the cube piece with folded edges meeting in the center; whipstitch in place.

STEP 11. Tie a bow using each piece of ribbon. Hand-stitch a ribbon bow and silver button to the top of each corner to finish. ■

Let's Fly a Kite
Continued from page 36

Cloud
Cut 2 white print
(reverse 1)
Add seam allowance when cutting for hand appliqué.

By Michele Crawford

Quick Quilter's Vest

Proudly exhibit your love for quilting when wearing this simple-to-make quilted vest.

BEGINNER SKILL

SPECIFICATIONS
Vest Size: Size varies

Block Size: 3 1/2" x 3 1/2"

Number of Blocks: 6

MATERIALS
- ☐ Purchased vest pattern
- ☐ 1/6 yard rose print
- ☐ 1/4 yard tan print
- ☐ 1/4 yard light gold print
- ☐ 1/2 yard button stripe
- ☐ 1 yard single-face quilted muslin
- ☐ 1 yard sewing print
- ☐ 1 spool each tan and ecru all-purpose thread
- ☐ 1 spool dark pink quilting thread
- ☐ 5" ecru Battenburg lace heart
- ☐ 5" x 5" square fusible transfer web
- ☐ 1/3 yard 3/8"-wide tan grosgrain ribbon
- ☐ 6 (5/8") wood buttons
- ☐ Thimble and scissors buttons
- ☐ Basic sewing supplies and tools

INSTRUCTIONS
STEP 1. Cut two vest fronts and a vest back from single-face quilted muslin. Trim seam allowance to 1/4".

STEP 2. To make Pinwheel blocks, cut 12 squares each rose and tan prints 2 5/8" x 2 5/8". Cut each square in half on one diagonal to make 24 triangles from each print. Sew a rose print triangle to a tan print triangle along diagonal seams to make triangle/squares as shown in Figure 1; repeat for 24 units. Press seams toward rose print.

STEP 3. Join two triangle/squares as shown in Figure 2; repeat for 12 units. Join two units as shown in Figure 3 to make a block; repeat for six blocks.

Figure 1
Make triangle/square as shown.

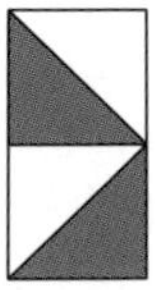

Figure 2
Join 2 triangle/squares to make a unit.

STEP 4. Join three Pinwheel blocks to

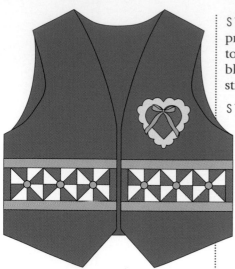

Quick Quilter's Vest
Placement Diagram
Size Varies

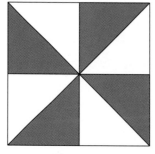

Pinwheel
3 1/2" x 3 1/2" Block

make a row; repeat. Cut four strips 1 1/4" x 4" rose print. Sew a strip to each end of a block row as shown in Figure 4; press seams toward strips. Repeat for second row.

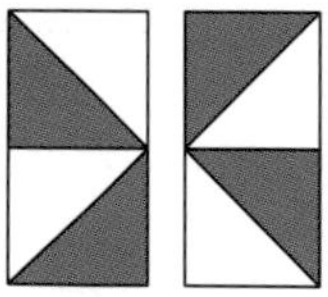

Figure 3
Join 2 units to make a Pinwheel block.

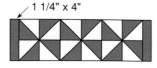

1 1/4" x 4"

Figure 4
Sew a 1 1/4" x 4" strip to each end of a block row.

STEP 5. Cut four strips light gold print 1 1/2" x 12 1/2". Sew a strip to the top and bottom of each block row; press seams toward strips.

STEP 6. Place a pieced strip across each vest front base 2 5/8" down from armhole as shown in Figure 5; pin in place. Topstitch using a 1/8" seam allowance to hold in place.

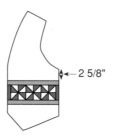

2 5/8"

Figure 5
Place pieced strip on vest front 2 5/8" down from armhole.

STEP 7. Cut two 6 1/2" x 12" rectangles from sewing print. Sew one rectangle to the bottom of the stitched row on each vest front base; press piece toward vest bottom. Topstitch around vest bottom to hold in place; trim excess fabric below vest front base as shown in Figure 6.

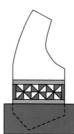

Figure 6
Trim excess fabric below vest front base.

STEP 8. Cut two 12" x 14" rectangles button stripe. Sew one rectangle to the top of the stitched row on each vest front base; press piece toward vest top. Topstitch around vest top to hold in place; trim excess fabric above vest front base.

STEP 9. Sew a wood button in the center of each Pinwheel block using dark pink quilting thread. Hand-quilt on light gold print strips 1/4" from seams using dark pink quilting thread. Machine-quilt top and bottom sections of vest fronts using ecru thread.

STEP 10. Sew the pieced vest fronts together with the vest back at side and shoulder seams. Press seams open.

STEP 11. Cut two vest fronts and a vest back from sewing print for lining. Sew together at side and shoulder seams; press seams open. Pin lining to stitched vest with wrong sides together, matching seams.

STEP 12. Cut four strips light gold print 1 1/4" by fabric width. Sew short ends together to make one long strip for binding. Press one long edge under 1/4". Sew around outside of vest and armholes. Turn binding to vest lining; hand-stitch in place.

STEP 13. Using lace heart as a pattern, trace inside heart on paper using a pencil; cut out. Cut a 5" x 5" square rose print. Fuse the square to the square of fusible transfer web following manufacturer's instructions. Trace heart shape on paper side of fused square; cut out. Remove paper backing.

STEP 14. Center fabric heart on lace heart; fuse in place. Center lace heart on left vest front. Topstitch lace heart in place using ecru thread. Satin-stitch around fused fabric heart using ecru thread.

STEP 15. Tie a bow using tan grosgrain ribbon. Stitch bow to top of fabric heart. Hand-stitch the thimble and scissors buttons to center of bow to finish. ■

By Vou Best

Evening Song

It is always challenging to make novelty or directional prints work to your advantage in a design. The Indian-girl print used in this quilted banner is a good example.

ADVANCED BEGINNER SKILL

SPECIFICATIONS
Banner Size: 19" x 36"

MATERIALS
- ☐ 1 yard Indian-girl print
- ☐ 1 strip sky-print fabric to match Indian-girl print 2 1/2" by fabric width
- ☐ 1 strip each purple and yellow prints 2 1/2" by fabric width
- ☐ 2 strips each purple and yellow prints 2 7/8" by fabric width
- ☐ Backing 23" x 40"
- ☐ Batting 23" x 40"
- ☐ 3 1/2 yards self-made or purchased binding
- ☐ Neutral color all-purpose thread
- ☐ 1 spool gold metallic thread
- ☐ Conchos, ribbon or leather for ties and beads for embellishments
- ☐ Basic sewing supplies and tool

INSTRUCTIONS

STEP 1. Pin a 2 7/8"-wide yellow print strip right sides together with a 2 7/8"-wide purple print strip; repeat with second set of strips. Mark a line every 2 7/8"; you will need 16 marked segments. Mark a diagonal line on each 2 7/8" segment referring to Figure 1.

STEP 2. Cut strips apart at 2 7/8" marks. Sew 1/4" on each side of the diagonal line on each layered square as shown in Figure 2. Cut squares apart on drawn diagonal line as shown in Figure 3 to make triangle/squares. You will need 32 triangle/squares.

Figure 1
Pin 2 7/8"-wide yellow and purple print strips right sides together. Mark a line every 2 7/8"; mark a diagonal line in each segment.

Figure 2
Sew 1/4" on each side of diagonal line.

Figure 3
Cut apart on drawn diagonal line.

Evening Song Banner
Placement Diagram
19" x 36"

3" x 19"

1 1/2" x 30"

2" x 30"

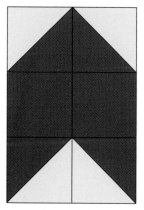

Arrow Block
4" x 6"

STEP 3. Cut a 2 1/2"-wide purple print strip into two 21"-long strips. Place the two strips right sides together; sew along one long edge; press seam open. Cut into 2 1/2" segments as shown in Figure 4; you will need eight segments.

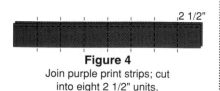

2 1/2"

Figure 4
Join purple print strips; cut into eight 2 1/2" units.

STEP 4. Repeat Step 3 using 2 1/2"-wide yellow print strip to make six yellow rectangle units.

STEP 5. Join two triangle/ square units on the yellow print sides as shown in Figure 5; repeat for eight units. Join two triangle/ square units on the purple print sides, again referring to Figure 5; repeat for eight units.

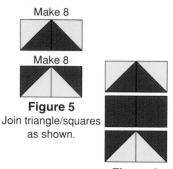

Make 8

Make 8

Figure 5
Join triangle/squares
as shown.

Figure 6
Join pieced units as shown to
make an Arrow block.

STEP 6. Join the pieced units as shown in Figure 6 to make an Arrow block; repeat for eight Arrow blocks.

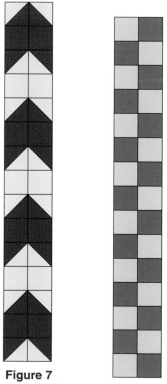

Figure 7
Join Arrow blocks
with yellow
rectangle units to
make a row.

Figure 8
Join units to
make a strip as
shown.

STEP 7. Join three Arrow blocks with three yellow rectangle units as shown in Figure 7 to make a strip; repeat for second strip. Press seams in one direction.

STEP 8. Cut 15 squares 2 1/2" x 2 1/2" Indian-girl print, keeping girls standing straight and upright. Cut 15 squares 2 1/2" x 2 1/2" sky-print fabric. ***Note:*** *Sky fabric in sample has color gradations from yellow through peach to purple.*

STEP 9. Sew a sky-print square to the left side of an Indian-girl print square; repeat for eight units. Sew a sky-print square to the right side of an Indian-girl print square; repeat for seven units; press seams toward Indian-girl print squares.

STEP 10. Join units pieced in Step 9 to make a strip as shown in Figure 8; press.

STEP 11. Cut two strips along length of Indian-girl print in the border area of the print 2 1/2" x 30 1/2". Sew a strip to each side of the stitched strip. Sew an Arrow-block strip to each side of the pieced section, positioning arrows referring to the Placement Diagram; press.

STEP 12. Cut two strips along length of Indian-girl print in the border area of the print 2" x 30 1/2". Sew a strip to opposite sides of the section; press seams toward strips.

STEP 13. Cut two strips Indian-girl print 3 1/2" x 19 1/2". Sew a strip to the top and bottom of the pieced section; press seams toward strips.

STEP 14. Prepare for quilting referring to General Instructions. Hand- or machine-quilt using gold metallic thread.

STEP 15. Finish edges as in General Instructions.

STEP 16. Embellish as desired using conchos, beads, leather strips, etc. ■

Twelve Days of Christmas Quilting

Add a touch of Christmas cheer to your home this season with these festive projects: quick and easy ornaments, holiday mantel covers, beautiful quilts, fun wearables, Christmas stockings and more. You'll want to spend many more than 12 days quilting for Christmas.

By Marian Shenk

Wreaths in the Attic Window

Placing a wreath in each window has become a holiday tradition. These pieced wreaths, enhanced by shiny snowflakes, decorate their own attic window.

INTERMEDIATE SKILL

SPECIFICATIONS

Quilt Size: 32" x 32"

Block Size: 12" x 12"

Number of Blocks: 4

MATERIALS

- ☐ 1/8 yard light green print for leaves
- ☐ 1/4 yard dark green print for wreaths
- ☐ 1/4 yard each medium and dark red prints for blocks
- ☐ 1/2 yard cream-on-cream print for background
- ☐ 1 yard border stripe
- ☐ Backing 36" x 36"
- ☐ Batting 36" x 36"
- ☐ 2 yards 1 1/4"-wide red plaid ribbon
- ☐ 12 (3/8") red wooden beads
- ☐ 60 (1/8") red wooden beads
- ☐ 60 plastic iridescent snowflakes
- ☐ Basic sewing supplies and tools and wash-out marker or pencil

INSTRUCTIONS

STEP 1. Prepare templates using pattern pieces given. Cut as directed on each piece for one block; repeat for four blocks.

STEP 2. To piece one block, sew a cream-on-cream print A to a green print A; repeat for four units. Join two units with B as shown in Figure 1; repeat for two units. Sew B to opposite sides of C.

Join two A-B units with a C-B unit as shown in Figure 2. Sew D and DR to left side of each pieced unit to complete one block as shown in Figure 3; repeat for four blocks.

Figure 1
Sew an A unit to each
short end of B.

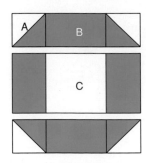

Figure 2
Sew 2 A-B units together
with 1 B-C unit.

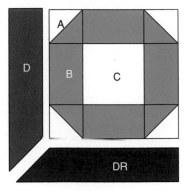

Figure 3
Sew D and DR to left
side of pieced section.

STEP 3. Cut two strips 1 1/2" x
12 1/2", three strips 1 1/2" x
25 1/2" and two strips 1 1/2" x
27 1/2" cream-on-cream print.

STEP 4. Join two blocks with
one 1 1/2" x 12 1/2" strip to make

1 1/2" x 12 1/2"

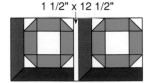

Figure 4
Join 2 blocks with 1 strip
to make a block row.

1 1/2" x 25 1/2"

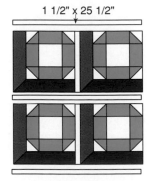

Figure 5
Join 2 rows with 3 strips as shown.

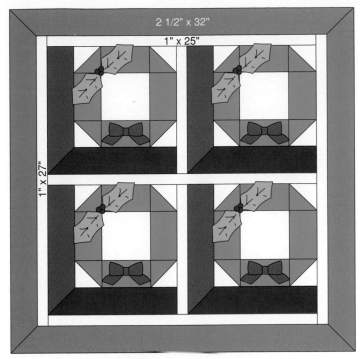

Wreaths in the Attic Window
Placement Diagram
32" x 32"

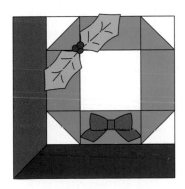

Attic Window Wreath
12" x 12" Block

a row as shown in Figure 4; repeat
for two rows. Press seams toward
strips.

STEP 5. Join two rows with
three 1 1/2" x 25 1/2" strips as
shown in Figure 5.

STEP 6. Sew a 1 1/2" x 27 1/2"
cream print strip to opposite sides
of pieced center.

STEP 7. Cut four strips border
print 3" x 32 1/2". *Note: If your
border stripe is narrower or wider
than the size given, cut your strips the
width of your border stripe.* Center
border strips on sides to make
accurate corners. Sew a strip to

each side, mitering corners; press
seams toward strips.

STEP 8. Hand-stitch snowflakes
to wreath section of each block
using 15 snowflakes per block.
Sew a 1/8" red bead in the center
of each snowflake.

STEP 9. Layer two leaf pieces
right sides together. Stitch all
around. Cut a 1" slit in one leaf
piece only. Turn right side out
through slit; press flat. Repeat for
eight leaves. Hand-stitch two
leaves to each wreath on dotted
lines marked on template referring
to the Placement Diagram for
positioning. Sew three large wood-
en beads where two leaves meet.

STEP 10. Cut four 18" lengths
red plaid ribbon. Make four bows.
Stitch bows to bottom of each
wreath.

STEP 11. Prepare quilt for quilting and finish as in General
Instructions, using quilting design
given, binding edges with self-
made or purchased binding. ∎

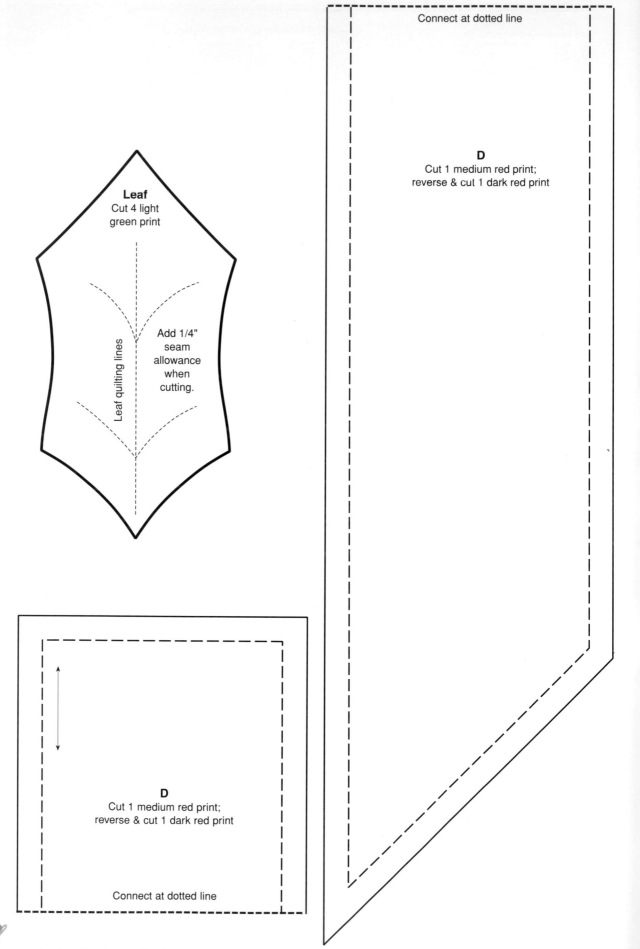

Leaf
Cut 4 light
green print

Leaf quilting lines

Add 1/4"
seam
allowance
when
cutting.

D
Cut 1 medium red print;
reverse & cut 1 dark red print

Connect at dotted line

D
Cut 1 medium red print;
reverse & cut 1 dark red print

Connect at dotted line

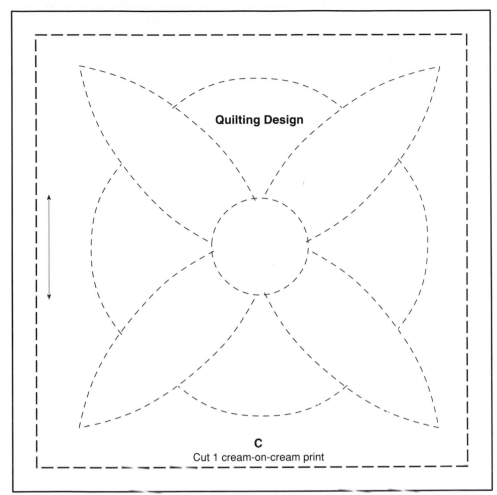

Quilting Design

C
Cut 1 cream-on-cream print

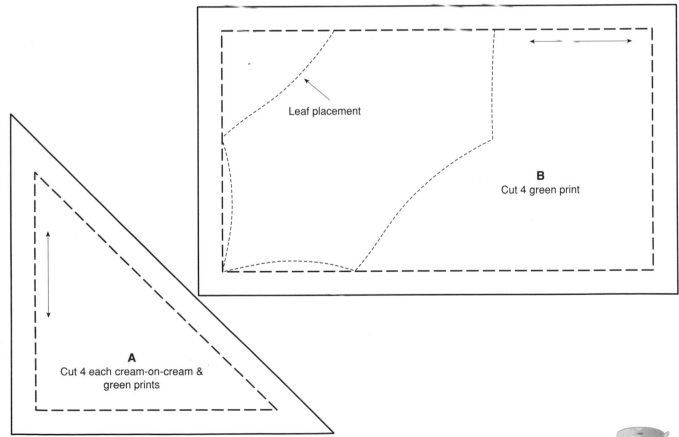

Leaf placement

B
Cut 4 green print

A
Cut 4 each cream-on-cream &
green prints

By Kate Laucomer

Fireside Stars

Stars and Christmas—they still just seem to go together as they did that first Christmas night so long ago in Bethlehem.

INTERMEDIATE SKILL

SPECIFICATIONS
Mantel Cover Size: 9" drop x 9" deep x 63 long"

Block Size: Star 6 3/8" x 6 3/8"; Log Cabin 7 1/2" x 7 1/2"

Number of Blocks: 7 Star blocks; 4 Log Cabin blocks

MATERIALS
☐ 1/4 yard total green scraps
☐ 1/4 yard total burgundy scraps
☐ 1 1/2 yards total white-on-cream or cream-on-cream prints
☐ Backing 20" x 65"
☐ Batting piece A—9 1/2" x 65"
☐ Batting piece B—depth of mantel by width of mantel plus 1/2"
☐ 1 spool each burgundy and cream all-purpose thread
☐ 9 1/2" or larger bias-square ruler
☐ Basic sewing supplies and tools, rotary cutter, ruler and cutting mat

PROJECT NOTE
For the scrappy look, be sure you have enough scraps to equal the total yardage listed for each color.

MEASURING YOUR MANTEL
STEP 1. Measure length. Divide the length by 9 and round off to a whole number. Example: 64" divided by 9 equals 7.1, or 7. Make seven blocks for this mantel cover.

STEP 2. Measure depth from front to back. Write down the measurements. For the example, this might be 9" x 63" for a finished size.

Star Blocks
STEP 1. To make seven Star blocks, cut 28 squares 1 3/4" x 1 3/4" and 56 rectangles 1 1/2" x 1 3/4" cream. Cut 84 squares green 1 1/2" x 1 1/2" and 14 squares burgundy 3 3/4" x 3 3/4". Cut the burgundy squares in half on one diagonal to make 28 triangles.

STEP 2. Divide the cream rectangles into

Star
6 3/8" x 6 3/8" Block

two even piles. Now evenly divide the green squares into two piles.

STEP 3. With right sides together, place one cream rectangle right sides together with one green square as shown in Figure 1. Sew together along diagonal of green square.

STEP 4. Trim off small green triangle only, leaving 1/4" seam allowance as shown in Figure 2. Press green square to right side; repeat for 28 units and 28 reverse units as shown in Figure 3.

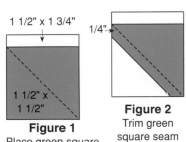

Figure 1
Place green square on background rectangle; stitch along diagonal.

1 1/2" x 1 3/4"

1 1/2" x 1 1/2"

1/4"

Figure 2
Trim green square seam allowance only.

Figure 3
Make 28 of each unit.

STEP 5. Divide cream squares, green squares, burgundy triangles and the rectangles with green points into seven piles. Join pieces as shown in Figure 4 to complete one block; repeat for seven blocks. *Note: Burgundy triangles are cut oversize; trimming will be necessary. Square up blocks to 6 7/8" x 6 7/8" as shown in Figure 5.*

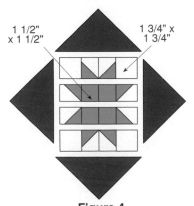

1 1/2" x 1 1/2"

1 3/4" x 1 3/4"

Figure 4
Piece 1 block as shown.

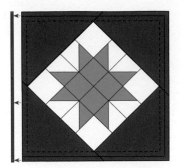

Figure 5
Square up blocks as shown.

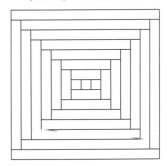

Log Cabin
7 1/2" x 7 1/2" Block

Log Cabin Blocks

STEP 1. Cut 20 strips 1" by fabric width and four squares 1" x 1" from cream-on-cream and/or white-on-cream prints.

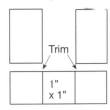

Trim

1" x 1"

Figure 6
Sew a strip to opposite sides of the 1" square.

STEP 2. Sew a strip to two opposite sides of a 1" square as shown in Figure 6; trim strips even with square. Press seams toward strips. Sew a strip to two remaining opposite sides; trim

and press. Continue adding strips to opposite sides until there are seven strips on each side of the center square; block should measure 8" x 8". Press and square up block. Repeat for four blocks.

STEP 3. Cut each block on the diagonal to make eight triangles referring to Figure 7.

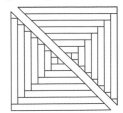

Figure 7
Cut Log Cabin block on the diagonal to make triangles.

PUTTING BLOCKS TOGETHER

STEP 1. Lay Star blocks out on point; place a Log Cabin triangle between each block as shown in Figure 8. Sew triangles to blocks; join pieced units to complete pieced front section. Press seams toward Star blocks.

STEP 2. Trim excess Log Cabin blocks even along top edge and on ends as shown in Figure 9.

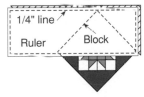

1/4" line

Ruler

Block

Figure 9
Trim Log Cabin blocks along top edge and ends as shown.

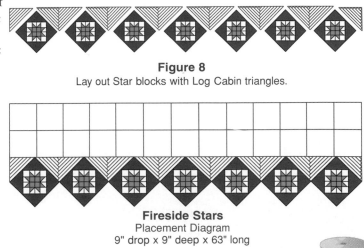

Figure 8
Lay out Star blocks with Log Cabin triangles.

Fireside Stars
Placement Diagram
9" drop x 9" deep x 63" long

Mantel Top & Finishing

STEP 1. Cut 26 squares 5 1/2" x 5 1/2" cream-on-cream and/or white-on-cream print. Join to make two 13-square rows; join rows. Trim off 3/4" from each end. *Note: The size of this piece will vary with the size of the mantel. Use the size of your mantel as measured in the beginning.*

STEP 2. Sew mantel top right sides together with pieced section along Log Cabin block edge; press seam open.

STEP 3. Place backing and mantel cover right sides together; pin. Turn over so backing is on top. Place batting piece A over pieced section part of cover; pin in place. Place batting piece B over mantel top section, leaving a 1/2" space between batting pieces. *Note: When batting is in two pieces with the space between, it allows the mantel cover to drape easily at edge of mantel.*

STEP 4. Turn so mantel cover

is on top; reposition pins so they are on this side. Trim edges even with mantel cover.

STEP 5. Starting on the straight edge, stitch around all sides, leaving an 8" opening on straight edge. Trim seam, clip corners and turn right side out. Press edges flat; slipstitch opening closed.

STEP 6. Using cream thread for cream background and burgundy thread for burgundy pieces, machine-quilt as desired. ■

By Beth Wheeler

Stained-Glass Window

Dress up a plain sweatshirt and be decked out for any holiday occasion.

PROJECT NOTES

The sample is a size extra-large and requires two strips of six blocks each around the hemline. A smaller sweatshirt may require fewer blocks. A larger sweatshirt may require the addition of border strips on each short end.

Seam allowances are 1/4" throughout unless otherwise specified.

INSTRUCTIONS

STEP 1. Cut one each 1 1/2" and 1 3/4" by fabric width strips from each of the five red-and-green prints and the main print. Cut all strips in half to make 22"-long strips; cut each strip in half again to make 11"-long strips.

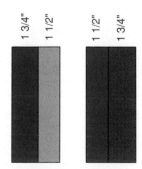

Figure 1
Pair 1 1/2"-wide A and B strips with remaining 1 3/4"-wide strips. Pair 1 3/4"-wide A and B strips with remaining 1 1/2"-wide strips.

INTERMEDIATE SKILL

SPECIFICATIONS
Shirt Size: Extra-large

Block Size: 4" x 4 1/2"

Number of Blocks: 12

MATERIALS
☐ Sweatshirt with set-in sleeves

☐ 1/8 yard each of 5 red-and-green prints (lightest fabric is A; darkest fabric is B)

☐ 5/8 yard main print for blocks and borders

☐ Neutral color all-purpose thread

☐ 1 spool monofilament

☐ Basic sewing supplies and tools, wash-out marker or pencil, rotary cutter, ruler and cutting mats

MAKE IT
QUICK!
24 HOURS
OR LESS!

Stained-Glass Window
Placement Diagram
Extra-Large

COLOR KEY
☐ Fabric A
■ Fabric B
☐ Fabric 1
■ Fabric 2
☐ Fabric 3
■ Fabric 4

STEP 2. Choose the lightest fabric for A and darkest fabric for B. Pair fabric strips referring to Figure 1, placing 1 3/4" strips of fabrics A and B with remaining 1 1/2" strips and placing 1 1/2" strips fabrics A and B with remaining 1 3/4" strips. Stitch pairs together along one long edge with right sides together; press seams in one direction.

STEP 3. Cut six 1 1/2" segments from each pair as shown in Figure 2.

1 1/2"

Figure 2
Cut strip sets in 1 1/2" segments.

STEP 4. Stitch segments together into three blocks each W, X, Y and Z as shown in Figure 3, noting especially the placement of fabrics A and B; press.

STEP 5. Stitch blocks into two long strips of six blocks each as shown in Figure 4; press.

STEP 6. Cut two strips main print 1 1/2" x 24 1/2". Press one long raw edge of each strip to wrong side 1/4". Sew the remaining raw edge of strips to one long edge on each block panel, trimming excess after stitching. Press seams toward strips.

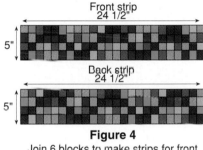

W
Make
3

X
Make
3

Y
Make
3

Z
Make
3

Figure 3
Join segments as shown
to make blocks.

Front strip
24 1/2"

5"

Back strip
24 1/2"

5"

Figure 4
Join 6 blocks to make strips for front
and back in order shown.

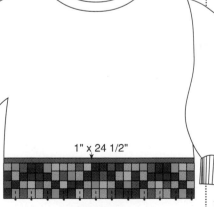

1" x 24 1/2"

Figure 5
Place pieced strip on bottom of
sweatshirt as shown.

STEP 7. Cut ribbing away from bottom of sweatshirt. Cut sweatshirt to desired length.

STEP 8. Match sweatshirt center front with center of one pieced and bordered strip. Pin toward sides with fold along top as shown in Figure 5. For extra-large sweatshirt, turn short ends under 1/2" at sides. For a smaller sweatshirt, cut excess off each end; turn under ends 1/2".

STEP 9. Repeat with remaining strip on sweatshirt back. Strips should meet at side seam, but should not overlap.

STEP 10. Zigzag along folded edges using monofilament in the top of the machine and all-purpose thread in the bobbin. Baste along hemline through all thicknesses.

STEP 11. Cut 2 1/2"-wide bias strips from main print. Stitch short ends together to make one 55"-long strip. Fold in half along length with wrong sides together; press along folded edge.

STEP 12. With raw edges together, stitched folded binding along hemline with a 3/8" seam allowance; trim excess. Fold binding to wrong side. Stitch in place by hand or machine.

STEP 13. Cut 2" x 2" squares from fabric scraps. Stitch these together to make two 2" x 24 3/4" strips for armholes; press under 1/2" along all edges.

STEP 14. Position a strip on sleeve side along shoulder seam, beginning and ending at under arm seam. Short ends should be spaced 1/2" apart to allow for any stretch needed in the underarm.

STEP 15. Stitch strips in place as in Step 10. Steam-press the entire sweatshirt for a crisp-looking finish. ■

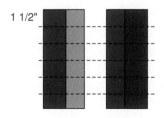

By Marian Shenk

Holly Bells

Dress up your mantel this year with this pretty appliquéd bell cover. Make matching Christmas stockings using coordinating fabrics and one of the stocking patterns in this book.

INTERMEDIATE SKILL

SPECIFICATIONS
Quilt Size: 18" x 49"

Block Size: 7" x 7"

Number of Blocks: 7

MATERIALS
- ☐ 1/8 yard green solid
- ☐ 1/2 yard green print
- ☐ 1 1/2 yards red print
- ☐ 6" x 8" piece gold lamé
- ☐ 12" x 12" piece cream-with-gold print
- ☐ Backing 22" x 54"
- ☐ Batting 22" x 54"
- ☐ 4 1/4 yards self-made or purchased binding
- ☐ All-purpose thread to match fabrics
- ☐ 1 spool off-white quilting thread
- ☐ 1 1/2 yards 3/4"-wide red plaid ribbon
- ☐ 6 gold 1/4"-diameter bells
- ☐ 3 (1 1/2") gold bells
- ☐ 1/2 yard 1/8" gold cording
- ☐ Basic sewing supplies and tools and wash-out marker or pencil

INSTRUCTIONS
STEP 1. Cut two strips red print 1 1/2" x 49 1/2" from length of fabric; set aside.

STEP 2. Prepare template for A triangle. Cut as directed on A.

STEP 3. Sew a green print A to a red print A along diagonals to make a square; repeat for 28 triangle/squares.

STEP 4. To make Block 1, join four A-A units as shown in Figure 1; press. Repeat for three blocks.

Figure 1
Join 4 A-A units to complete 1 block; make 3.

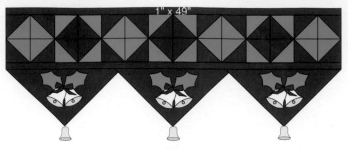

Holly Bells Mantel Cover
Placement Diagram
18" x 49"

Block 1
7" x 7"
Make 3

Block 2
7" x 7"
Make 4

hand-stitch in place under bell center. Stitch remaining bell edge in place. Repeat for three bells.

STEP 12. Cut red plaid ribbon into three 18" pieces; tie a bow with each piece. Tack bow in place at top of appliquéd bells; trim ribbon ends and adjust size of bow as necessary.

STEP 13. Pin triangles in place along bottom edge of previously stitched block piece, overlapping points as necessary to fit as shown in Figure 4. Stitch in place.

Figure 4
Pin triangles to pieced section,
overlapping points as needed to fit.
Continued on page 69

STEP 5. To make Block 2, join four A-A units as shown in Figure 2; press. Repeat for four blocks.

Figure 2
Join 4 A-A units to
complete 1 block; make 4.

STEP 6. Arrange the blocks as shown in Figure 3; join together to make a long row.

STEP 7. Sew a 1 1/2" x 49 1/2" red print strip to each long side of pieced row. Press seams toward strips.

Figure 3
Join blocks to make a row.

STEP 8. Cut two squares red print 12 7/8" x 12 7/8". Cut each square in half on one diagonal to make four triangles. Set aside one triangle for another project.

STEP 9. Prepare templates for appliqué pieces using full-size drawing given for design. Cut as directed, adding a 1/8"–1/4" seam allowance all around when cutting each piece.

STEP 10. Center and pin appliqué pieces on large triangles using full-size pattern drawing as a guide for overlapping and order of stitching.

STEP 11. Hand-appliqué pieces in place using thread to match fab-

rics and turning under seam allowance as you stitch. Before stitching bottom edge of bell over inside bell pieces, cut six pieces cording 3" long. Thread end of one piece through one small bell;

Leaf quilting lines

⑥

Bell
Cut 6 cream-with-gold print

Inside Bell
Cut 6 gold lamé

①
③
④
②

Leaf
Cut 6 green solid

⑤

By Norma Storm

Patchwork Tablecloth

Round up all your red, green and white Christmas prints to make this scrappy holiday tablecloth.

PROJECT NOTES

Because this tablecloth is not lined, all seams were overcast to prevent fraying. This may be done using a serger.

In the sample, one Four-Patch block was stitched in place facing the wrong direction. The Placement Diagram shows the proper placement. I wish I could say I did this on purpose, but it was purely accidental.

INSTRUCTIONS

STEP 1. Cut 4 1/2" x 4 1/2" squares from red fabrics as follows: 18 red 1; 16 red 2; 20 red 3; four red 4; and 12 red 5.

STEP 2. Cut 2 1/2" x 2 1/2" squares from green fabrics as follows: 32 green 1; 36 green 2; 14 green 3; 34 green 4; and 24 green 5.

STEP 3. Cut 2 1/2" x 2 1/2" squares from white fabrics as follows: 26 white 1; 34 white 2; 14 white 3; 34 white 4; and 32 white 5.

STEP 4. Remove selvage edges from the 2 1/4-yard piece of red solid. Cut into four 10 1/2"-wide lengthwise strips; set aside.

STEP 5. Sew a white square to a green square referring to Figure 1 for color combinations; repeat for all green and white squares; press seams toward green. Join two like-fabric square segments

BEGINNER SKILL

SPECIFICATIONS

Tablecloth Size: 58 1/2" x 74 1/2" with 9 1/4" border

Block Size: 4" x 4"

Number of Blocks: 70

MATERIALS

- ☐ 1/4 yard red 4
- ☐ 1/3 yard each reds 2 and 5
- ☐ 1/2 yard each reds 1 and 3
- ☐ 1/4 yard each 5 different green fabrics
- ☐ 1/4 yard each 5 different white fabrics
- ☐ 2 1/4 yards red solid for borders
- ☐ All-purpose thread to match fabrics
- ☐ Basic sewing supplies and tools, rotary cutter, ruler and cutting mat

9 1/4" x 40"

9 1/4" x 74"

Patchwork Tablecloth
Placement Diagram
58" x 74"

to make a Four-Patch unit, again referring to Figure 1 for color combinations and number of blocks of each combination. You will need 70 Four-Patch blocks. Press all blocks.

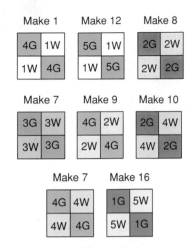

Figure 1
Make Four-Patch blocks in color combinations shown.

STEP 6. Arrange Four-Patch blocks with red squares in rows referring to Figure 2 for placement of blocks and squares. Join blocks in rows; join rows to complete pieced center. Press seams in one direction. *Note: All seams were sewn on a sewing machine using an overcast stitch to finish edges.*

STEP 7. Trim two 10 1/2" by fabric length red solid strips 40 1/2" long. Sew a strip to the top and bottom of the pieced center; press seams toward strips.

STEP 8. Trim the two remaining 10 1/2" by fabric length red solid strips 76 1/2" long. Sew a strip to opposite long sides; press seams toward strips.

STEP 9. Overcast outside edges of border strips. Turn 1" to wrong side all around; press. Stitch in place to finish edge. ■

1R	4G 2W / 2W 1G	2R	3G 3W / 3W 3G	3R	2G 2W / 2W 2G	4R	5G 1W / 1W 5G	1R	4G 1W / 1W 4G
2G 4W / 4W 2G	1R	4G 2W / 2W 4G	2R	3G 3W / 3W 3G	3R	2G 2W / 2W 2G	4R	5G 1W / 1W 5G	1R
5R	2G 4W / 4W 2G	1R	4G 2W / 2W 4G	2R	3G 3W / 3W 3G	3R	2G 2W / 2W 2G	4R	5G 1W / 1W 5G
1G 5W / 5W 1G	5R	2G 4W / 4W 2G	1R	4G 2W / 2W 4G	2R	3G 3W / 3W 3G	3R	2G 2W / 2W 2G	4R
3R	1G 5W / 5W 1G	5R	2G 4W / 4W 2G	1R	4G 2W / 2W 4G	2R	3G 3W / 3W 3G	3R	2G 2W / 2W 2G
5G 1W / 1W 5G	3R	1G 5W / 5W 1G	5R	2G 4W / 4W 2G	1R	4G 2W / 2W 4G	2R	3G 3W / 3W 3G	3R
2R	5G 1W / 1W 5G	3R	1G 5W / 5W 1G	5R	2G 4W / 4W 2G	1R	4G 2W / 2W 4G	2R	3G 3W / 3W 3G
4G 4W / 4W 4G	2R	5G 1W / 1W 5G	3R	1G 5W / 5W 1G	5R	2G 4W / 4W 2G	1R	4G 2W / 2W 4G	2R
1R	4G 4W / 4W 4G	2R	5G 1W / 1W 5G	3R	1G 5W / 5W 1G	5R	2G 4W / 4W 2G	1R	4G 2W / 2W 4G
1G 5W / 5W 1G	1R	4G 4W / 4W 4G	2R	5G 1W / 1W 5G	3R	1G 5W / 5W 1G	5R	2G 4W / 4W 2G	1R
3R	1G 5W / 5W 1G	1R	4G 4W / 4W 4G	2R	5G 1W / 1W 5G	3R	1G 5W / 5W 1G	5R	2G 4W / 4W 2G
2G 2W / 2W 2G	3R	1G 5W / 5W 1G	1R	4G 4W / 4W 4G	2R	5G 1W / 1W 5G	3R	1G 5W / 5W 1G	5R
5R	2G 2W / 2W 2G	3R	1G 5W / 5W 1G	1R	4G 4W / 4W 4G	2R	5G 1W / 1W 5G	3R	1G 5W / 5W 1G
1G 5W / 5W 1G	5R	2G 2W / 2W 2G	3R	1G 5W / 5W 1G	1R	4G 4W / 4W 4G	2R	5G 1W / 1W 5G	3R

Figure 2
Arrange blocks in rows with red squares as shown.

By Marian Shenk

Poinsettia Table Topper

Dress up your living room with this quilted coffee table cover decked out with poinsettia appliqués and a simple pieced Four-Patch block in the center.

INTERMEDIATE SKILL

SPECIFICATIONS
Table Cover Size: 13" x 27"

Block Size: 12" x 12"

Number of Blocks: 1

MATERIALS
- ☐ 1/8 yard gold lamé for block border
- ☐ 1/8 yard red print 2 for poinsettias
- ☐ 1/4 yard red print 1 for poinsettias and block triangles
- ☐ 1/2 yard light green print for background
- ☐ Scraps green for leaves and triangles
- ☐ Scrap yellow solid for poinsettia centers
- ☐ Batting 45" x 45"
- ☐ Lightweight batting 16" x 30"
- ☐ Backing 16" x 30"
- ☐ 1 spool each yellow, green and red all-purpose thread
- ☐ 1 spool contrasting quilting thread
- ☐ 1 package dark green wide bias tape
- ☐ Green embroidery floss
- ☐ Basic sewing supplies and tools and wash-out marker or pencil

INSTRUCTIONS
STEP 1. Prepare templates for all pattern pieces. Cut as directed on each piece, adding a 1/4" seam allowance to all appliqué pieces when cutting.

STEP 2. Sew a red print 1 A to a light green print A as shown in Figure 1; repeat for 12 units. Sew a green print A to a

light green print A; repeat for four units. Press seams toward darkest fabric.

Figure 1
Sew a red print A to a
light green print A.

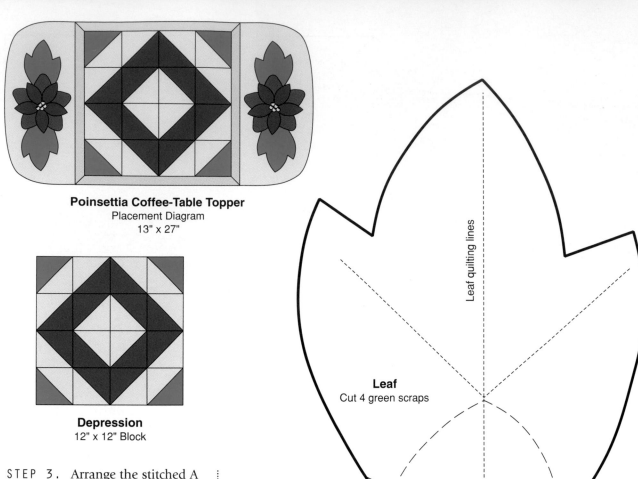

Poinsettia Coffee-Table Topper
Placement Diagram
13" x 27"

Depression
12" x 12" Block

Leaf quilting lines

Leaf
Cut 4 green scraps

STEP 3. Arrange the stitched A units in rows as shown in Figure 2; join units in rows. Join rows to complete one block; press.

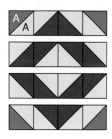

Figure 2
Arrange A units in rows as shown.

STEP 4. Cut four strips gold lamé 1" x 13 1/2". Sew a strip to each side of the pieced block, mitering corners; press.

STEP 5. Cut two pieces light green print 7 1/2" x 13 1/2". Sew a piece to two opposite sides of the pieced block; press seams toward added pieces.

STEP 6. Center and trace a poinsettia design on the light green

rectangles using full-size drawing of Poinsettia design and wash-out marker or pencil.

STEP 7. Pin a fabric leaf shape in place over traced design using lines on full-size pattern as a guide for placement. Hand-appliqué leaves in place using matching thread, turning under seam allowance when stitching.

STEP 8. Pin petal shapes on traced design, overlapping pieces as necessary. *Note: The top layer of petals shows the red print fabric used with wrong side facing to change the value of the color slightly.* Hand-appliqué pieces in place in numerical order using matching thread, turning under seam allowance when stitching.

STEP 9. Hand-appliqué flower

centers in place. Satin-stitch ends of centers using 3 strands green embroidery floss.

STEP 10. Round corners to make a pleasing shape, keeping all corners symmetrical.

STEP 11. Prepare for quilting and finish referring to General Instructions. ∎

HINT
When a slight value change is needed, it is not always necessary to purchase a different fabric. The wrong side of most fabrics is a different color than the right side. When a slight change in color is needed for shading, try using the wrong side of some of your fabrics.

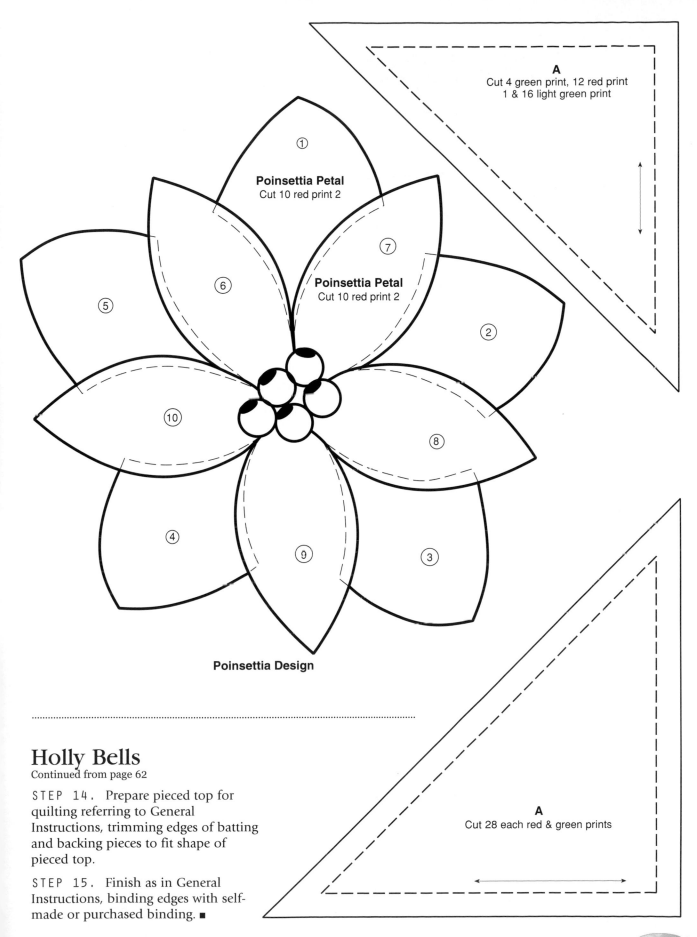

A
Cut 4 green print, 12 red print
1 & 16 light green print

① **Poinsettia Petal**
Cut 10 red print 2

⑦ **Poinsettia Petal**
Cut 10 red print 2

⑥ ⑤ ② ⑩ ⑧ ④ ⑨ ③

Poinsettia Design

A
Cut 28 each red & green prints

Holly Bells
Continued from page 62

STEP 14. Prepare pieced top for quilting referring to General Instructions, trimming edges of batting and backing pieces to fit shape of pieced top.

STEP 15. Finish as in General Instructions, binding edges with self-made or purchased binding. ∎

By Ann Boyce

Patchwork Ornaments

These simple patchwork ornaments use scraps of leftover fabrics and can be made up in bunches in an afternoon.

Stained-Glass

BEGINNER SKILL

SPECIFICATIONS
Ornament Size: 4 1/2" x
    4 1/2"

MATERIALS
☐ 1 (2" x 2") square purple, teal, red and yellow

☐ 1" x 28" strip black solid

☐ Batting 6" x 6"

☐ 5" x 5" square black solid for backing

☐ 8" black cording

☐ Polyester stuffing

☐ Neutral color all-purpose thread

☐ Basic sewing supplies and tools

INSTRUCTIONS
STEP 1. From the 1" x 28" strip black solid, cut two 2" strips, three 4" strips and two 5" strips.

STEP 2. Join two 2" x 2" colored squares with a 1" x 2" strip black solid; repeat. Press seams toward strips. Join the two pieced units with a 1" x 4" strip as shown in Figure 1; press.

STEP 3. Sew a 1" x 4" strip to opposite sides of the pieced unit; press seams toward strips. Sew a 1" x 5" strip to remaining sides; press seams toward strips.

STEP 4. Place pieced square on top of the batting piece. Machine-quilt through all layers in the ditch of seams or as desired. Trim batting even with edges of pieced top.

STEP 5. Pin both ends of cording at one corner of quilted top as shown in Figure 2. Place backing piece right sides together with quilted top and cording inside.

Stained-Glass
Placement Diagram
4 1/2" x 4 1/2"

1" x 4"

Figure 1
Join pieced units with
1" x 4" strip.

Figure 2
Pin cording at corner.

STEP 6. Stitch all around, leaving a 2" opening on one side. Clip corners; turn right side out. Fill with polyester stuffing. Hand-stitch opening closed to finish.

Cow Ornament

SPECIFICATIONS
Ornament Size: 4 1/2" x 4 1/2"

MATERIALS

☐ 2 (2" x 2") squares red and white solids

☐ 1 strip cow print 1 1/4" x 20"

☐ 5" x 5" square red solid for backing

☐ Batting 6" x 6"

☐ 8" red cording

☐ Polyester stuffing

☐ Neutral color all-purpose thread

☐ Basic sewing supplies and tools

INSTRUCTIONS

STEP 1. Sew a white square to a red square; press seams toward red. Repeat for second unit. Join the two units to make a Four-Patch block referring to the Placement Diagram.

Cow Ornament
Placement Diagram
4 1/2" x 4 1/2"

STEP 2. From the 1 1/4" x 22" strip cow print, cut two 3 1/2" and two 5" strips. Sew shorter strips to two opposite sides of Four-Patch unit. Sew longer strips to remaining sides; press all seams toward strips.

STEP 3. Finish as in Steps 4–6 for Stained-Glass Ornament.

Piped Four-Patch

INSTRUCTIONS

STEP 1. Join a light square with a contrasting square with gold piping between seams as shown in Figure 3; repeat. Join the two pieced units with piping between seams.

Piped Four-Patch
Placement Diagram
4" x 4"

Figure 3
Join 2 squares with piping between.

SPECIFICATIONS
Ornament Size: 4" x 4"

MATERIALS

☐ 2 squares light print 2 1/2" x 2 1/2"

☐ 2 squares contrasting print 2 1/2" x 2 1/2"

☐ Batting 6" x 6"

☐ Backing 4 1/2" x 4 1/2"

☐ 8" gold cording

☐ 1 package gold piping

☐ Polyester stuffing

☐ Neutral color all-purpose thread

☐ Basic sewing supplies and tools

STEP 2. Machine-baste piping around outside edges of stitched unit, beginning and ending at a corner and overlapping ends.

STEP 3. Finish as in Steps 4–6 for Stained-Glass Ornament.

Diamond Drop

INSTRUCTIONS

STEP 1. Prepare template for A; cut as directed on piece.

STEP 2. Join pieces along side

Diamond Drop
Placement Diagram
Approximately 2 1/2" x 4 1/2"

seams, leaving a 1 1/2" opening in one seam and inserting cording in seam at tip.

SPECIFICATIONS
Ornament Size: Approximately 2 1/2" x 4 1/2"

MATERIALS

☐ Scraps 4 Christmas prints 3" x 7"

☐ 8" white cording

☐ Polyester stuffing

☐ Neutral color all-purpose thread

☐ Basic sewing supplies and tools

STEP 3. Clip corners; turn right side out. Fill with polyester stuffing. Hand-stitch opening closed to finish.

Santa Diamonds

SPECIFICATIONS
Ornament Size: 4" x 5"

MATERIALS

☐ Scrap Santa print 6" x 8"

☐ Scrap bridal/prom dress fabrics 4" x 6"

☐ Batting 6" x 6"

☐ Batting 6" x 6"

☐ 8" white cording

☐ Polyester stuffing

☐ Neutral color all-purpose thread

☐ Basic sewing supplies and tools

INSTRUCTIONS

STEP 1. Prepare template for pieces B and C. Cut as directed on pieces.

STEP 2. Sew B to C as shown in

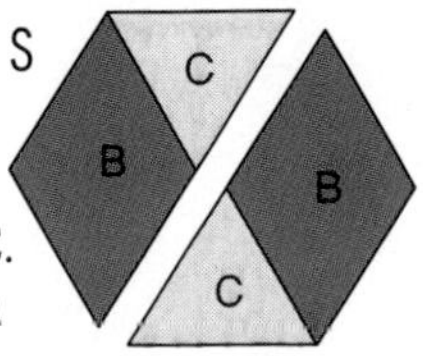

Figure 4
Join B and C pieces as shown.

Figure 4; repeat. Join the two pieced units to make a hexagon-shaped piece; press.

STEP 3. Finish as in Steps 4–6 for Stained-Glass Ornament except center cording on one C piece instead of at a corner.

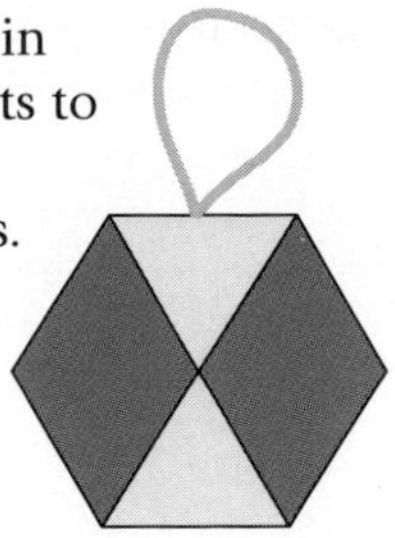

Santa Diamonds
Placement Diagram
4" x 5"

Lamé Star
INSTRUCTIONS

STEP 1. Cut interfacing into two 3" x 3" squares; fuse a square to the wrong side of each 3" x 3" lamé square.

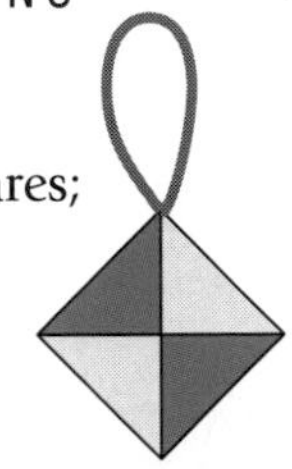

STEP 2. Cut each

Lamé Star
Placement Diagram
Approximately 3 1/2" x 3 1/2"

fused square in half on one diagonal to make triangles. Sew a blue triangle to a silver triangle as

BEGINNER SKILL

SPECIFICATIONS
Ornament Size: 3 1/2" x 3 1/2"

MATERIALS

- ☐ 3" x 3" square silver lamé
- ☐ 3" x 3" square light blue lamé
- ☐ Backing 4" x 4"
- ☐ 3" x 6" piece cotton knit fusible interfacing
- ☐ 8" silver cording
- ☐ Polyester stuffing
- ☐ 1 (1 1/2") white-with-gold-trim embroidered star
- ☐ Neutral color all-purpose thread
- ☐ Basic sewing supplies and tools

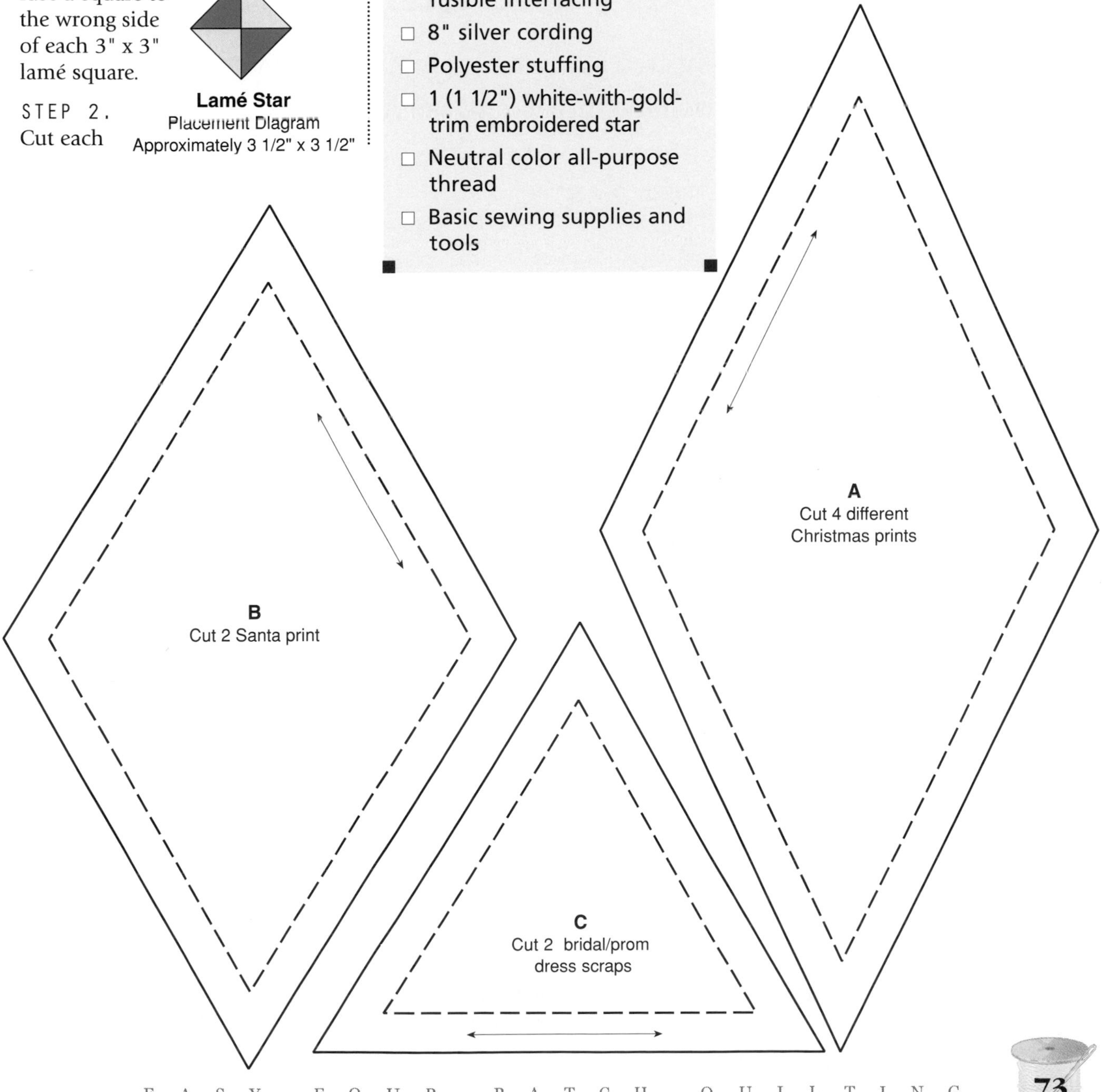

shown in Figure 5; repeat. Join the two units as shown in Figure 6 to make a square.

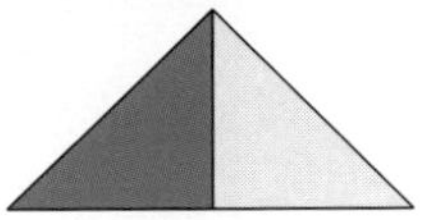

Figure 5
Sew a blue triangle to a silver triangle.

Figure 6
Join triangle units to make a square.

STEP 3. Sew the embroidered star to the center of the pieced square.

STEP 4. Finish as in Steps 2 and 3 for Diamond Drop Ornament. ■

B
Cut 2 Santa print

C
Cut 2 bridal/prom dress scraps

A
Cut 4 different Christmas prints

By Beth Wheeler

Golden Elegance

This elegant tree skirt and matching stocking use gold metallic thread and fancy stitches.

INTERMEDIATE SKILL

SPECIFICATIONS

Tree Skirt Size: 48 " x 48"
(point to point)

Stocking Size: 12" x 14"

Block Size: 12" x 12" (tree skirt);
5 3/4" x 5 3/4" (stocking)

Number of Blocks: 10 for tree skirt;
7 for stocking

MATERIALS
- [ ] 1/2 yard each 5 white-to-tan prints
- [ ] 1/2 yard cream print for stocking, backing and lining
- [ ] 1 3/4 yards tan-and-cream stripe

- [ ] Backing 52" x 52" for tree skirt
- [ ] 52" x 52" low-loft batting for tree skirt
- [ ] 17" x 15" low-loft batting for stocking
- [ ] 8 gold-metallic 3 1/2" tassels
- [ ] 7 yards gold-metallic double-fold bias tape
- [ ] Neutral color all-purpose thread
- [ ] 7" piece 1/4" gold braid, ribbon or cording
- [ ] 1 spool gold-metallic thread
- [ ] 1 spool clear monofilament
- [ ] Basic sewing supplies and tools, rotary cutter, ruler and cutting mat

Tree Skirt

STEP 1.   From each of the five white-to-tan prints and tan-and-cream stripe, cut one strip 1 1/4", 1 1/2", 1 3/4" and 2" wide. Cut two additional strips of each width, choosing fabric randomly for each strip. You will need eight strips of each width.

STEP 2. Stitch strips together along length as shown in Figure 1, arranging strips randomly according to width and color to make a 36 1/2" x 42" strip set. Press seam allowances all in one direction.

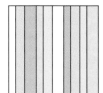

Figure 1
Stitch strips together to make strip set; press seam allowances in 1 direction.

STEP 3. Cut 40 squares 4 3/4" x 4 3/4" from stitched strip set as shown in Figure 2.

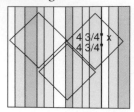

Figure 2
Cut squares on the bias.

STEP 4. Stitch four squares together to make a Four-Patch unit as shown in Figure 3; press. Repeat for 10 Four-Patch units.

Figure 3
Join 4 squares to make a
Four-Patch unit.

STEP 5. Cut 20 squares tan-and-cream stripe 6 7/8" x 6 7/8" on the bias. Cut each square in half on the diagonal with the stripe as shown in Figure 4 to make 40 triangles.

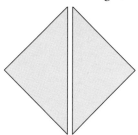

Figure 4
Cut stripe square in half on
the diagonal following
stripes of fabric.

STEP 6. Stitch four triangles and one Four-Patch unit together to make a block as shown in Figure 5; repeat for eight blocks. Press seams toward triangles.

STEP 7. Stitch a triangle to two adjacent sides of one Four-Patch unit as shown in Figure 6; repeat. Press seams toward triangles.

STEP 8. Sew two triangles together as shown in Figure 7; repeat. Press seams in one direction.

Golden Elegance Tree Skirt
Placement Diagram
48" x 48"

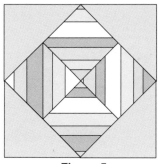

Figure 5
Join 1 Four-Patch unit and 4
triangles to make a block.

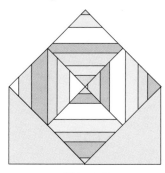

Figure 6
Join 1 Four-Patch unit and
2 triangles as shown.

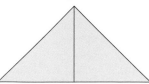

Figure 7
Join 1 stripe triangles as shown.

STEP 9. Arrange stitched blocks and units in rows as shown in Figure 8. Join units in rows; join rows and add triangles, again referring to Figure 8, to complete front panel. Press seams in one direction.

Figure 8
Arrange pieced units in rows as shown.

STEP 10. Layer pieced top with batting and prepared backing piece.

STEP 11. Prepare for quilting and quilt referring to the General Instructions. *Note: The tree skirt was quilted using machine decorative stitches with gold metallic thread in the top of the machine and all-pur-*

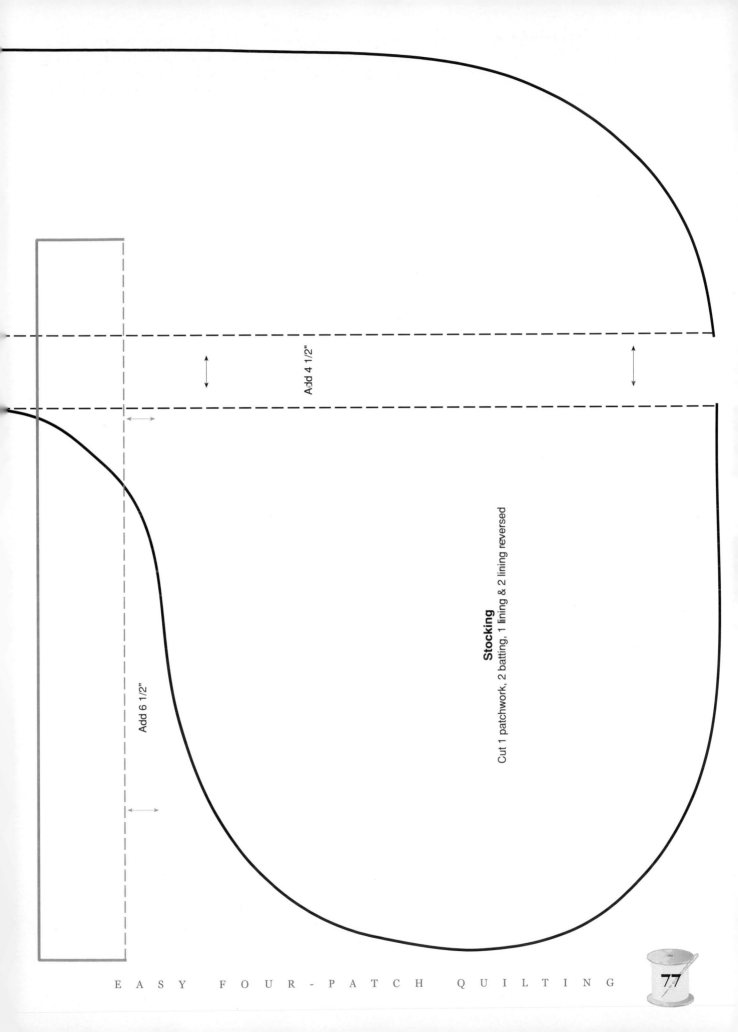

Stocking

Cut 1 patchwork, 2 batting, 1 lining & 2 lining reversed

Add 4 1/2"

Add 6 1/2"

pose thread in the bobbin. Trim edges even with pieced top.

STEP 12. Fold quilted tree skirt to find center point. Cut a circle to fit your tree and an opening as shown in Figure 9.

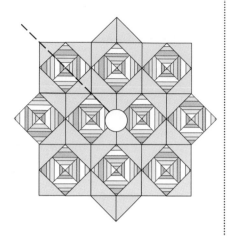

Figure 9
Cut on opening and circle for tree trunk.

STEP 13. Bind edges with gold metallic double-fold bias tape referring to the General Instructions.

STEP 14. Hand-stitch one tassel on each point, except half points at opening, to finish.

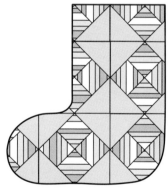

Golden Elegance Stocking
Placement Diagram
12" x 14"

Stocking

STEP 1. From each of the five-white-to-tan prints and tan-and-cream stripe, cut one strip each, 1 1/4", 1 1/2" and 1 3/4" wide. Cut all strips in half to make 22" long.

STEP 2. Stitch strips together to make a strip set as shown in Figure 1, arranging strips randomly according to width and color. Press seam allowances all in one direction.

STEP 3. Cut 28 squares 2 1/2" x 2 1/2" from stitched strip set as shown in Figure 2.

STEP 4. Stitch four squares together to make a Four-Patch unit as shown in Figure 3; repeat for seven Four-Patch units.

STEP 5. Cut 14 squares tan-and-cream stripe 3 5/8" x 3 5/8" fabric. Cut each square in half on the diagonal with the stripe on the bias as shown in Figure 4 to make 28 triangles.

STEP 6. Stitch four triangles and one Four-Patch unit together to make a block as shown in Figure 5; repeat for seven blocks. Press seams toward triangles.

STEP 7. Stitch blocks together to make a panel as shown in Figure 10.

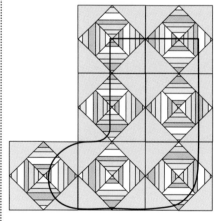

Figure 10
Stitch blocks together
as shown.

STEP 8. Place tracing paper over Stocking pattern on page 78. Trace and cut out.

STEP 9. Place pattern on pieced panel, again referring to Figure 10; cut one for front. Cut two from batting and three from lining, reversing two pieces.

STEP 10. Layer one batting piece with front. Quilt as desired by hand or machine with gold-metallic thread. Layer remaining batting piece with one reversed cream print piece for stocking back; quilt as desired.

STEP 11. Place front and back right sides together; stitch around outside using a 1/2" seam allowance, leaving top open. Stitch cream print lining pieces together using a 1/2" seam allowance, leaving top open. Clip corners; press seams.

STEP 12. Slip lining inside quilted shell, wrong sides together; baste around top opening.

STEP 13. Fold 7" piece of ribbon, braid or cording in half for a loop. Place inside stocking with ends even with back seam allowance of stocking. Stitch in place inside seam allowance.

STEP 14. Cut a 6" x 16" piece of tan-and-cream stripe for the cuff. Stitch together along short ends with right sides together using a 1/2" seam allowance; press seam allowances open.

STEP 15. Fold cuff in half with wrong sides together as shown in Figure 11. Slip cuff inside stocking, with raw edges matching and seam allowance of cuff matching back seam allowance of stocking. Stitch around top using a 1/2" seam allowance. Fold cuff to right side, encasing all raw edges.

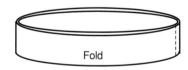

Fold

Figure 11
Fold cuff in half, with wrong
sides together.

STEP 16. Stitch tassel at seam on cuff. ∎

By Sherry Reis

Star of Bethlehem

A striking medallion quilt is created using a
simple pieced block and a plain block.

CUTTING
White-on-White Print
STEP 1. Cut four strips 2 1/2" x 42 1/2" for
borders.

STEP 2. Cut four srips 5 1/2" by fabric width;
subcut into 5 1/2" square segments for B. You will
need 24 B squares.

STEP 3. Cut five strips 3 3/8" by fabric width;
subcut into 3 3/8" square segments. Cut each
square on one diagonal to make 120 A triangles.

STEP 4. Cut eight squares 1 1/2" x 1 1/2" for C.

Red Print
STEP 1. Cut four strips along length 1 1/2" x
46 1/2".

STEP 2. Cut four strips from remaining
width of fabric 5 7/8" by fabric width. Subcut
into 5 7/8" square segments to make 20 squares.
Cut each square in half on one diagonal for D
triangles.

STEP 3. Cut eight squares 1 1/2" x 1 1/2" for C.

STEP 4. Cut six strips 2" by fabric width for binding.

Green Print
STEP 1. Cut four strips 1 1/2" x 40 1/2" for
borders.

STEP 2. Cut two strips 3 3/8" by fabric width ;
subcut into 3 3/8" square segments. Cut each
square in half on one diagonal to make 40 triangles
for A.

STEP 3. Cut eight squares
1 1/2" x 1 1/2" for C.

INTERMEDIATE SKILL

SPECIFICATIONS
Quilt Size: 48" x 48"

Block Size: 2" x 2" and
5" x 5"

Number of Blocks: 4 small
and 40 large

MATERIALS
- [ ] 1/2 yard green print
- [ ] 1 3/8 yards red print
  (includes binding)
- [ ] 1 1/2 yards white-on-
  white print
- [ ] Backing 52" x 52"
- [ ] Batting 52" x 52"
- [ ] Backing 45" x 45"
- [ ] Neutral color
  all-purpose thread
- [ ] Quilting thread
- [ ] Basic sewing supplies
  and tools.

PIECING

STEP 1. Sew a green print A to a white-on-white print A to make a square. Sew one white-on-white A to two adjacent green sides of the pieced square as shown in Figure 1. Sew D to the pieced unit to complete Flying Goose block as shown in Figure 2; repeat for 40 blocks.

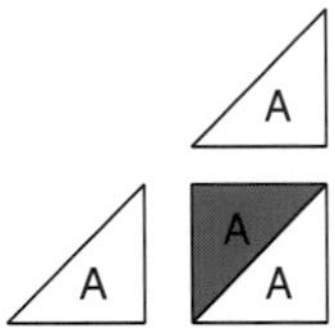

Figure 1
Join A units as shown.

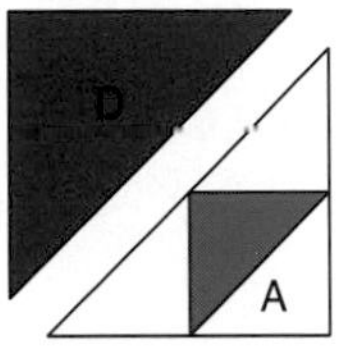

Figure 2
Sew D to the A unit to complete Flying Goose block.

STEP 2. Sew a red print C to a white-on-white print C. Join a white-on-white print C and a green print C. Join the two pieced C units as shown in Figure 3 to make a Four-Patch block; repeat for four blocks.

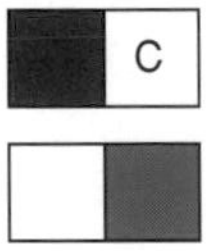

Figure 3
Join 2 pieced C units to make a Four-Patch block.

STEP 3. Arrange the Flying Goose blocks with B as shown in Figure 4. Join blocks to make rows; join rows to complete pieced center. Press seams in one direction.

Star of Bethlehem
Placement Diagram
48" x 48"

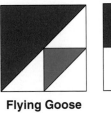

Flying Goose
5" x 5" Block
Make 40

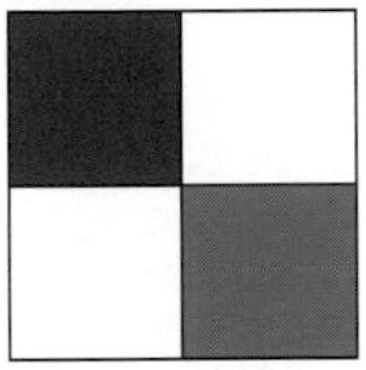

Four-Patch
2" x 2" Block
Make 4

Figure 4
Arrange Flying Goose blocks with piece B in rows.

STEP 4. Referring to Figure 5 for adding all borders, sew a 1 1/2" x 40 1/2" green print strip to opposite sides of pieced center; press seams toward strips. Sew a red C square

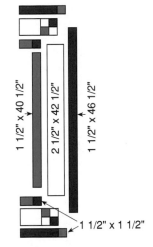

Figure 5
Add borders in order shown.

to each end of the remaining two 1 1/2" x 40 1/2" strips; sew a strip to remaining opposite sides. Press seams toward strips.

STEP 5. Sew a 2 1/2" x 42 1/2" white-on-white print strip to opposite sides of pieced center; press seams toward strips. Sew a Four-Patch block to each end of the remaining two 2 1/2" x 42 1/2" strips; sew a strip to remaining opposite sides. Press seams toward strips.

STEP 6. Sew a 1 1/2" x 46 1/2" red print strip to opposite sides of pieced center; press seams toward strips. Sew a green C square to each end of the remaining two 1 1/2" x 46 1/2" strips; sew a strip to remaining opposite sides. Press seams toward strips.

STEP 7. Prepare top for quilting and finish referring to General Instructions, making binding from previously cut 2"-wide red strips. ∎

By Holly Daniels

Poinsettia Christmas

Decorate your bedroom with this lovely quilt combining Carrie Nation blocks with button-accented poinsettias.

INTERMEDIATE SKILL

SPECIFICATIONS
Quilt Size: 84" x 108"

Block Size: 12" x 12"

Number of Blocks: 48

MATERIALS
- [ ] 1/2 yard red print 2
- [ ] 2 1/2 yards green print
- [ ] 2 5/8 yards red print 1
- [ ] 4 1/2 yards white solid
- [ ] Backing 88" x 112"

- [ ] Batting 88" x 112"
- [ ] 11 yards self-made or purchased binding
- [ ] Neutral color all-purpose thread
- [ ] 1 spool red rayon thread
- [ ] 1 yard fusible transfer web
- [ ] 1 yard fabric stabilizer
- [ ] 18 (1") gold buttons or gold fabric-covered buttons
- [ ] 1 spool quilting thread
- [ ] Basic sewing supplies and tools, rotary cutter, ruler and cutting mat

INSTRUCTIONS
STEP 1. Cut 16 strips each green print and white solid 3 1/2" by fabric width. Sew a green strip to a white strip to make a strip set; press seams toward green. Cut strip set at 3 1/2" segments to make 192 segments. Join two segments to make a Four-Patch unit as shown in Figure 1; make 96.

STEP 2. Cut 19 strips each red print 1 and white solid 2" by fabric width. Sew a red strip to a white strip to make a strip set; press seams toward red. Repeat for all strips. Cut strips into 2" segments to make 384 segments. Join two segments to make a Four-Patch unit as shown in Figure 2; make 192.

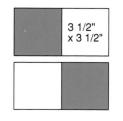

3 1/2"
x 3 1/2"

Figure 1
Join 2 segments to make a
Four-Patch unit.

2"
x 2"

Figure 2
Join 2 segments to
make a Four-Patch unit.

STEP 3. Cut 16 strips white solid 3 1/2" by fabric width. Sew the red Four-Patch units to the strips as shown in Figure 3; press seams toward strips. Cut apart as shown in Figure 4. Join two of these segments to make another Four-Patch unit as shown in Figure 5; repeat for 96 units.

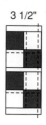

3 1/2"

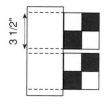

Figure 3
Sew red Four-Patch units to a white strip.

Figure 4
Cut apart as shown.

Figure 5
Join 2 segments to make a Four-Patch unit.

STEP 4. Sew two green-and-white units and two red-and-white units together to make a block as shown in Figure 6; repeat for 48 blocks. Press all blocks.

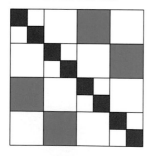

Figure 6
Join Four-Patch units to complete 1 block.

STEP 5. Join four blocks to make larger squares as shown in Figure 7; press. Repeat for 12 blocks.

STEP 6. Bond fusible transfer web to the wrong side of red print 2. Prepare template for petal using

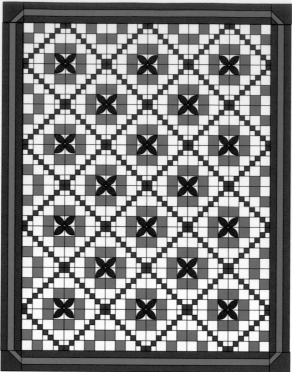

Poinsettia Christmas Quilt
Placement Diagram
84" x 108"

Corner Block
6" x 6" Block
Make 4

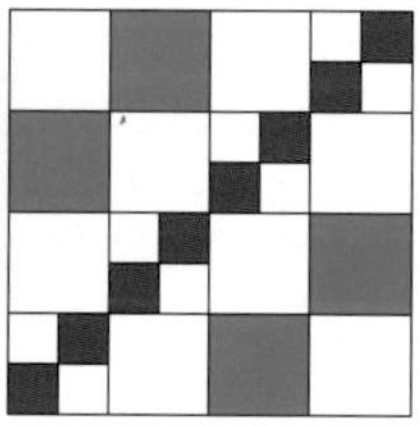

Carrie Nation
12" x 12" Block
Make 48

pattern piece given. Trace 72 petal shapes onto paper side of fused fabric; cut out on traced lines. Remove paper backing.

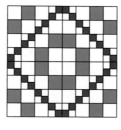

Figure 7
Join 4 blocks to make a larger square.

STEP 7. Fuse four petals to the center of each large square formed in Step 5 as shown in Figure 8. Place a piece of fabric sta-

bilizer behind each petal. Using red rayon thread in the top of the machine and

Figure 8
Fuse 4 petal shapes to the center of the larger square.

all-purpose thread in the bobbin, satin-stitch around each petal; remove stabilizer.

STEP 8. Join three large squares together to make a row; repeat for four rows. Join rows to complete pieced center.

STEP 9. Machine-appliqué remaining petals in place in open areas formed when rows are joined.

STEP 10. Cut 18 strips red print 1 and nine strips green print 2 1/2" by fabric width. Cut one green and two red strips at 22" intervals. Stitch together as shown in Figure 9 to make longer strips; press seams open. Stitch a green strip between two red strips, staggering seams as shown in Figure 10. Press seams in one direction.

STEP 11. Sew one extra-long strip set to long sides of pieced center; press seams toward strips. Trim top and bottom ends even with pieced center.

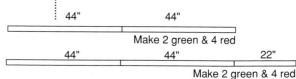

44"   44"
Make 2 green & 4 red

44"   44"   22"
Make 2 green & 4 red

Figure 9
Join strips on short ends to make longer strips.

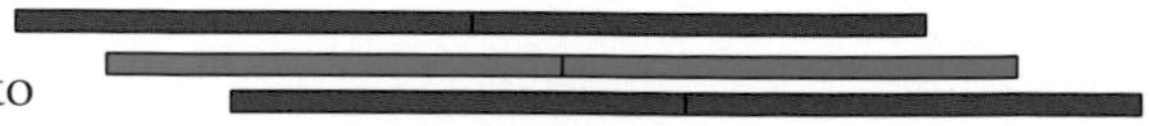

Figure 10
Stitch a green strip between 2 red strips, staggering seams as shown.

STEP 12. Prepare A, B and C templates for corner blocks. Cut as directed on each piece. Sew C to B

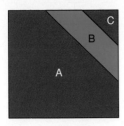

Figure 11
Sew C to B to A to make corner block.

and B-C to A to complete one block as shown in Figure 11; repeat for four blocks. Press seams in one direction. Repeat for four strip sets.

STEP 13. Cut remaining border strip sets 72 1/2" long. Sew a corner block to each end as shown in Figure 12. Sew these strips to the top and bottom of pieced center with A on the outside edge. Press seams toward strips.

STEP 14. Prepare top for quilting

and binding referring to General Instructions.

Figure 12
Sew a corner block to each end of red/green/red strip.

STEP 15. Hand-stitch a gold button to the center of each petal unit to finish. ∎

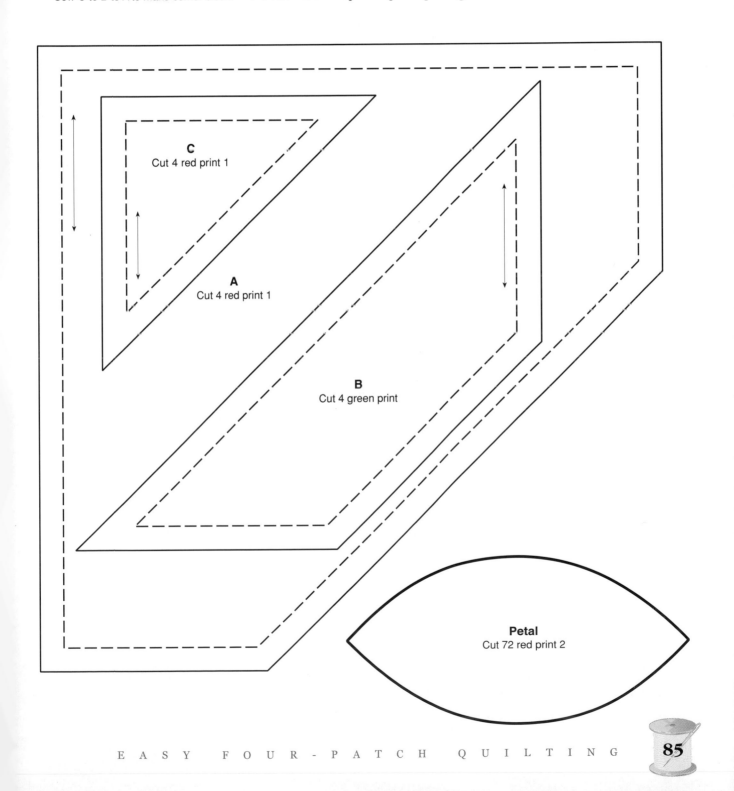

C
Cut 4 red print 1

A
Cut 4 red print 1

B
Cut 4 green print

Petal
Cut 72 red print 2

FOUR-PATCH
FAVORITES

It's amazing that such a simple block can create truly dynamic quilts! In this chapter you'll find glorious quilts of all sizes. Some quilts are complex and for experienced quilters only. Others are quick and easy to complete, but have an added twist to give them an original look. Whether you want a modern three-dimensional look or a traditional baby quilt, you'll find designs here to inspire you to start a quilt today.

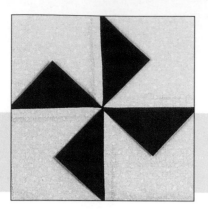

By Lucy A. Fazely

Folded Pinwheel Quilt

Children and adults alike will be fascinated with the three-dimensional triangles on this colorful quilt.

MATERIALS

- ☐ 1/2 yard each mottled gold, orange, purple, blue and green
- ☐ 1 yard mottled red
- ☐ 2 1/2 yards white solid
- ☐ Backing 50" x 62"
- ☐ Batting 50" x 62"
- ☐ Neutral color all-purpose thread
- ☐ Basic sewing supplies and tools

INSTRUCTIONS

STEP 1. Cut 11 strips white solid 3 1/2" by fabric width; cut into 3 1/2" square segments. You will need 128 squares.

STEP 2. Cut six strips white solid 6 1/2" by fabric width; cut into 6 1/2" square segments. You will need 31 squares.

STEP 3. From each of the six mottled colors, cut four strips 3 1/2" by fabric width. Set aside two strips of each color for prairie point border. From remaining strips, cut 3 1/2" square segments. You will need 20 squares each gold, orange, purple and blue and 24 squares each red and green.

STEP 4. Fold each of the colored squares in half on one diagonal; fold again to make a smaller triangle as shown in Figure 1.

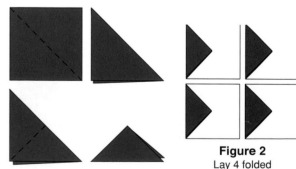

Figure 1
Fold triangle to make a prairie point.

Figure 2
Lay 4 folded triangles on 4 white squares as shown.

STEP 5. To make one block, lay four same-colored folded triangles on four 3 1/2" x 3 1/2" white solid squares as shown in Figure 2; pin triangles in place.

STEP 6. Arrange squares in a pinwheel shape as shown in Figure 3. Join two squares together; repeat. Join the pieced units to complete one block as shown in Figure 4; press seams away from points. Make five blocks each gold, orange, purple and blue and six blocks each red and green.

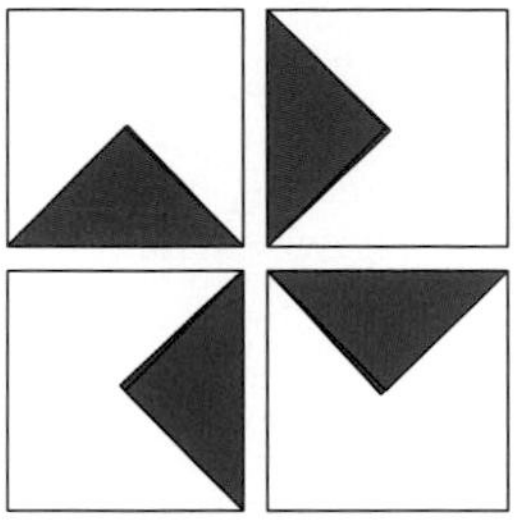

Figure 3
Arrange squares in pinwheel shapes.

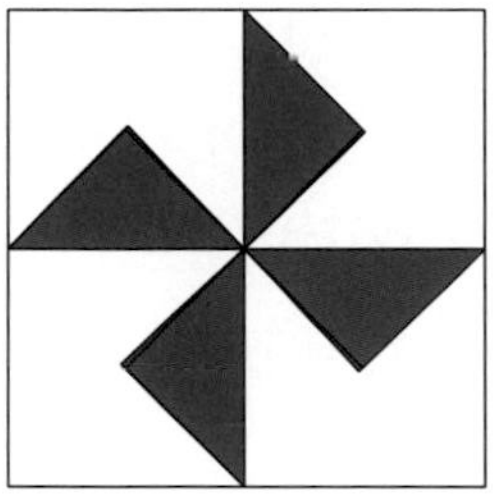

Figure 4
Join pieced units to complete 1 block.

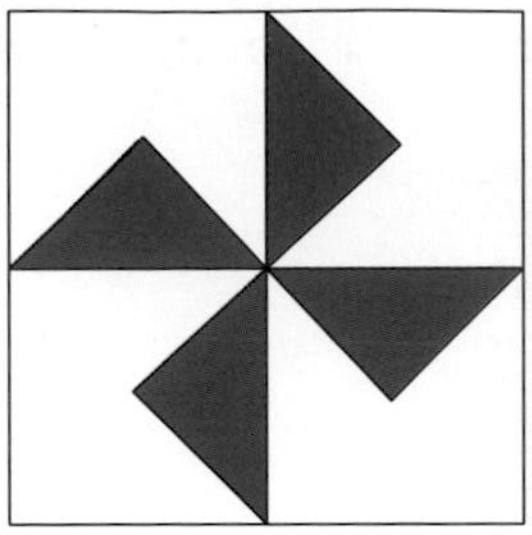

Folded Pinwheel
6" x 6" Block

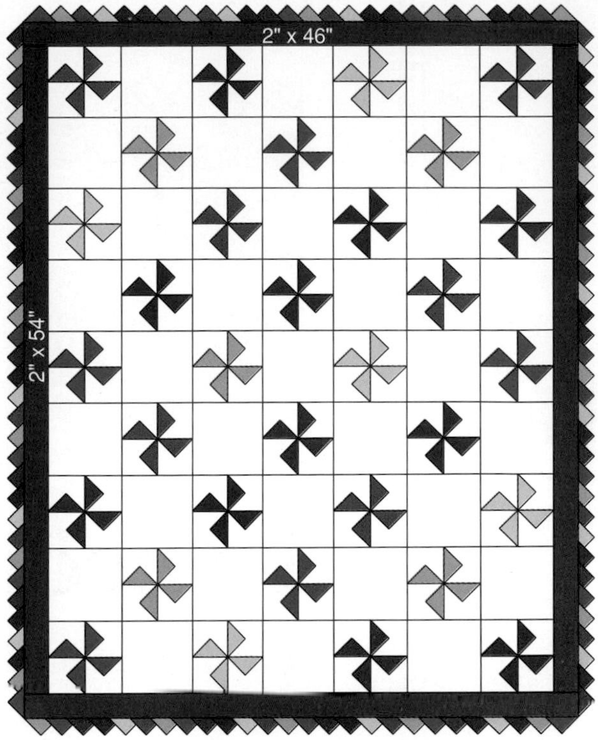

Folded Pinwheel Quilt
Placement Diagram
46" x 58" (without prairie points)

STEP 7. Join four pieced blocks with three 6 1/2" x 6 1/2" squares white solid to make a row as shown in Figure 5; press seams in one direction. Repeat for five rows.

STEP 8. Join three pieced blocks with four 6 1/2" x 6 1/2" squares white solid to make a row as shown in Figure 6; press seam in the opposite direction as rows in Step 7. Repeat for four rows.

STEP 9. Join rows to complete pieced center referring to the Placement Diagram and photo for arrangement. Press seams in one direction.

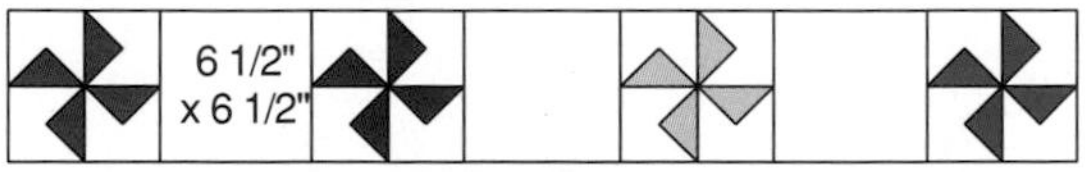

Figure 5
Join 4 blocks with 3 squares to make a row.

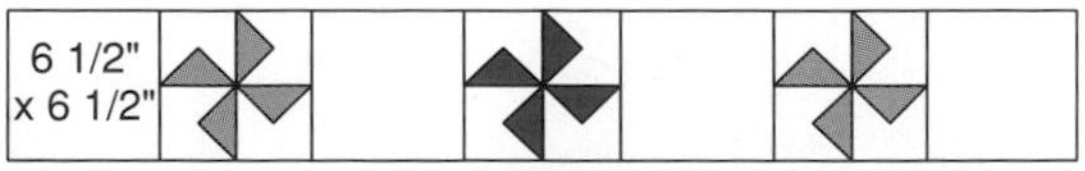

Figure 6
Join 3 blocks with 4 squares to make a row.

STEP 10. Cut and piece two border strips each 2 1/2" x 54 1/2" and 2 1/2" x 46 1/2" from mottled red fabric.

STEP 11. Sew longer strips to opposite long sides of pieced center; press seams toward strips. Repeat with remaining strips on top and bottom.

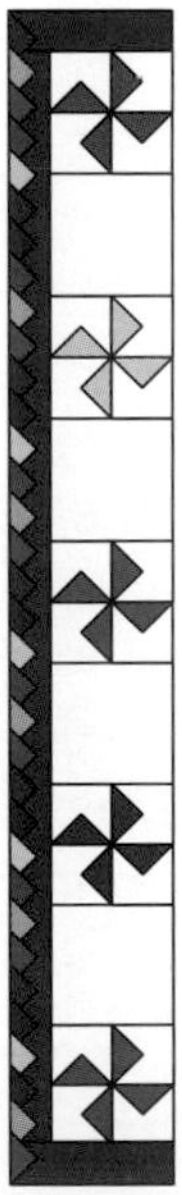

Figure 7
Arrange 34 prairie points along long edge as shown.

STEP 12. From the remaining 3 1/2" by fabric width strips, cut 20 squares of each color. Fold squares to make prairie points as in Step 4. Pin 34 prairie points on each long side of quilt top, nestling points inside one another and facing toward center of quilt as shown in Figure 7. Repeat with 26 prairie points on top and bottom edges.

STEP 13. Lay batting on large, flat surface; center backing right side up on top of batting. Center quilt top right side down on backing; pin around all edges.

STEP 14. Sew all around edges, leaving a 12" opening on one side. Trim corners and excess backing and batting. Turn right side out through opening; pull out corners and press edges flat. Hand-stitch opening closed.

STEP 15. Quilt as desired by hand or machine. ■

By Sue Harvey

Ramblin' Rose

This is an original variation of an old quilt design recognized by many names—Old Maid's Ramble, Double X's or Fox and Geese. It dates to around 1885. A design is formed not by the blocks themselves but by the placement of fabrics in the corners of the blocks.

INTERMEDIATE SKILL

SPECIFICATIONS

Quilt Size: 57" x 81"

Block Size: 6" x 6"

Number of Blocks: 96

MATERIALS

- ☐ 1/2 yard green plaid
- ☐ 1/2 yard green print
- ☐ 1/2 yard rose print (or enough to cut 156 B triangles)
- ☐ 1/2 yard vine print (or enough to cut 156 B triangles)
- ☐ 1 yard burgundy plaid
- ☐ 1 1/4 yards gold plaid
- ☐ 4 yards off-white print
- ☐ Backing 61" x 85"
- ☐ Batting 61" x 85"
- ☐ 8 yards self-made or purchased binding
- ☐ Coordinating all-purpose thread
- ☐ Basic sewing supplies and tools and template plastic

PROJECT NOTE

It is important to carefully choose the fabric for the rose square inside the green square and the vine square inside the burgundy star. The fabrics must have a design that will form a rose and a vine from the corner triangles when four blocks are combined.

INSTRUCTIONS

STEP 1. Cut two 3 1/2" x 72 1/2" and two 3 1/2" x 48 1/2" border strips along the length of the off-white print; set aside.

STEP 2. Prepare templates using pattern pieces given. Cut as directed on each piece, carefully placing B triangles on rose and vine fabrics as shown in Figure 1.

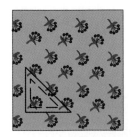

Figure 1
Carefully place B triangle pattern on rose and vine fabrics as shown.

Ramblin' Rose
Placement Diagram
57" x 81"

Ramblin' Rose
6" x 6" Block

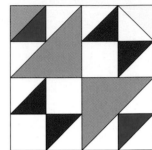

Corner Block
6" x 6"

Edge 1 Block
6" x 6"

Edge 2 Block
6" x 6"

COLOR KEY
- ☐ Off-white print
- Gold plaid
- Green plaid
- Burgundy plaid
- Green print
- Rose print
- ☐ Vine print

STEP 3. Sew pieces together to make units referring to Figure 2 and the Color Key. Press all units.

STEP 4. Join pieced units to make Ramblin' Rose, Corner, Edge 1 and Edge 2 blocks referring to Figure 3 for positioning of units and number of each block to make. Press all blocks.

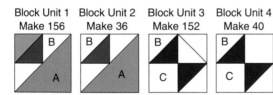

Block Unit 1
Make 156

Block Unit 2
Make 36

Block Unit 3
Make 152

Block Unit 4
Make 40

Figure 2
Join pieces to make block units as shown.

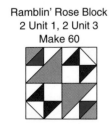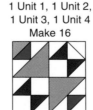

Ramblin' Rose Block
2 Unit 1, 2 Unit 3
Make 60

Corner Block
1 Unit 1, 1 Unit 2,
2 Unit 4
Make 4

Edge 1 Block
1 Unit 1, 1 Unit 2,
1 Unit 3, 1 Unit 4
Make 16

Edge 2 Block
1 Unit 1, 1 Unit 2,
1 Unit 3, 1 Unit 4
Make 16

Figure 3
Combine block units to
make blocks as shown.

CB	E1	E2	E1	E2	E1	E2	CB
E2							E1
E1							E2
E2							E1
E1							E2
E2							E1
E1							E2
E2							E1
E1							E2
E2							E1
E1							E2
CB	E2	E1	E2	E1	E2	E1	CB

Figure 4
Arrange blocks in 12 rows of 8 blocks each,
placing each block as shown.

CB—Corner Block
E1—Edge 1 Block
E2—Edge 2 Block
Unmarked blocks are Ramblin' Rose blocks.

STEP 5. Arrange blocks in 12 rows of eight blocks each referring to Figure 4 and the Placement Diagram for positioning of blocks. Join blocks in rows; join rows to complete pieced center. Press all seams.

STEP 6. Referring to Figure 5 and Color Key, make four corner units and 180 B-B units; press.

Corner Unit
Make 4

B-B Units
Make 180

Figure 5
Combine pieces to make border unit as shown.

STEP 7. Sew the 3 1/2" x 72 1/2" strips cut in Step 1 to opposite long sides of the pieced center; press seams toward strips.

STEP 8. Sew a corner unit to each end of the 3 1/2" x 48 1/2" border strips cut in Step 1 as shown in Figure 6; press. Sew these strips to the top and bottom of the pieced center; press seams toward strips.

STEP 9. Join 26 B-B units as shown in Figure 7; repeat to make two 26-unit X border strips. Join 19 B-B units, again referring to Figure 7, to make two 19-unit X border strips.

STEP 10. Join 26 B-B units as shown in Figure 8; repeat to make two 26-block Y border strips. Join 19 B-B units, again referring to Figure 8, to make two 19-unit Y border strips.

STEP 11. Join one 26-unit X border strip with one 26-unit Y border strip as shown in Figure 9; repeat. Sew the pieced strips to opposite long sides of the pieced top; press seams toward inner border strips.

STEP 12. Join one 19-unit X border strip with one 19-unit Y border strip again referring to Figure 9;

3 1/2" x 48 1/2"

Figure 6
Sew a corner unit to each end of a 3 1/2" x 48 1/2" border strip as shown.

Figure 7
Join B-B units to make X border strip as shown.

Figure 8
Join B-B units to make Y border strip as shown.

Figure 9
Join X and Y border strips as shown.

repeat. Sew the pieced strips to the top and bottom of the pieced top; press seams toward inner border strips.

STEP 13. Prepare quilt for quilting and finish as in General Instructions, binding edges with self-made or purchased binding. ■

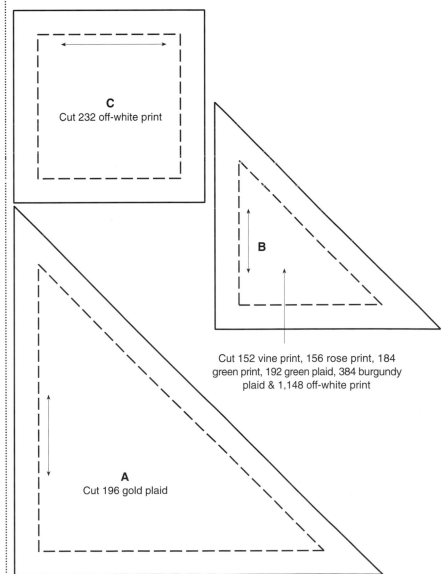

C
Cut 232 off-white print

B

Cut 152 vine print, 156 rose print, 184 green print, 192 green plaid, 384 burgundy plaid & 1,148 off-white print

A
Cut 196 gold plaid

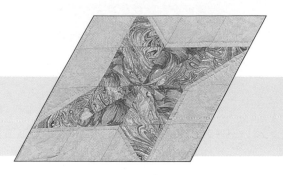

By Karen Combs

Clay's Choice

Combine your love of traditional quilt designs with the allure of illusions to create this intriguing wall quilt.

INTERMEDIATE SKILL

SPECIFICATIONS

Quilt Size: 27 1/2" x 29"

Block Size: 11 1/2" x 19 1/2" diamond

Number of Blocks: 3

MATERIALS

☐ 1/4 yard each light, medium and dark green mottled

☐ 1/4 yard each light blue 1, light blue 2, medium blue 1, medium blue 2, dark blue 1 and dark blue

2 mottled for blocks

☐ 1/2 yard medium blue 3 for inner border and background

☐ 1/2 yard dark blue 3 for outer border and binding

☐ Backing 32" x 32"

☐ Batting 32" x 32"

☐ 4 1/2 yards self-made or purchased binding

☐ Coordinating all-purpose thread

☐ 1 spool blue metallic thread

☐ Basic sewing supplies and tools

INSTRUCTIONS

STEP 1. Prepare templates using pattern pieces given. Cut as directed on each piece.

STEP 2. Cut two 6 3/8" x 11" rectangles medium blue 3. Cut into triangles as shown in Figure 1; set aside.

STEP 3. Cut four 3 1/2" x 3 1/2" squares light blue 2 for corners; set aside.

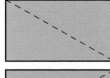

Figure 1
Cut 6 3/8" x 11" rectangles into triangles.

STEP 4. To piece one diamond block, join A, B and C pieces in rows as shown in Figure 2, referring to Figure 3 and Color Key for color placement.

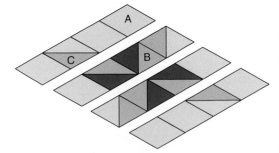

Figure 2
Join A, B and C pieces in rows.

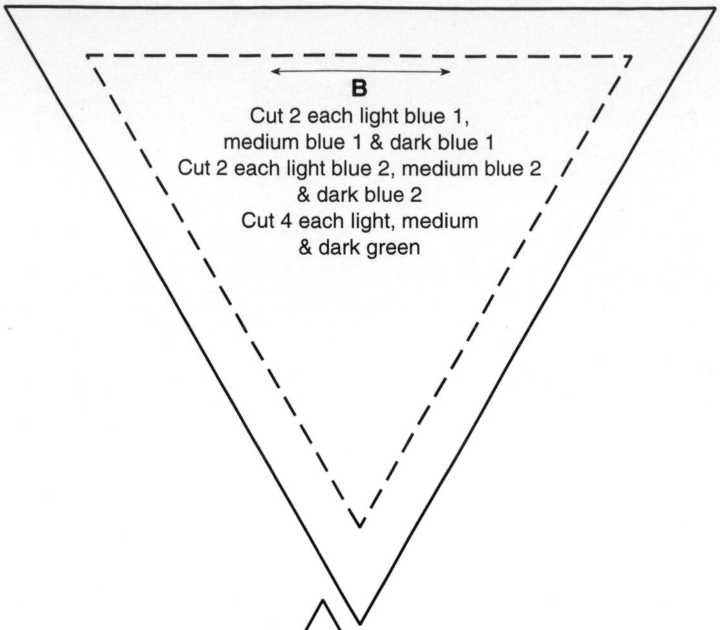

B

Cut 2 each light blue 1,
medium blue 1 & dark blue 1
Cut 2 each light blue 2, medium blue 2
& dark blue 2
Cut 4 each light, medium
& dark green

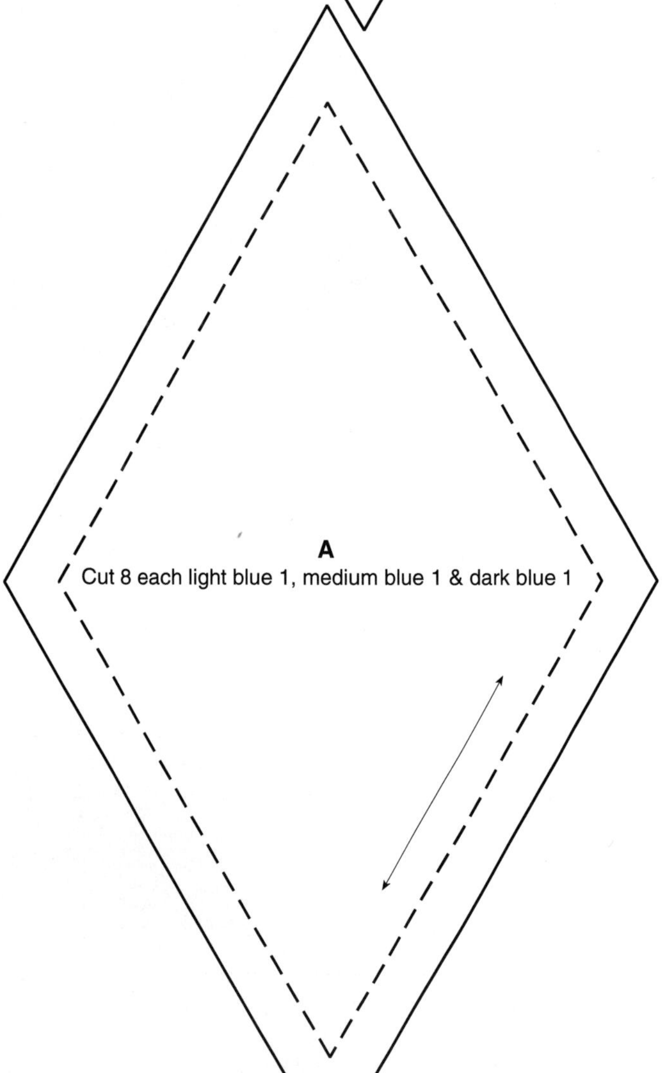

A

Cut 8 each light blue 1, medium blue 1 & dark blue 1

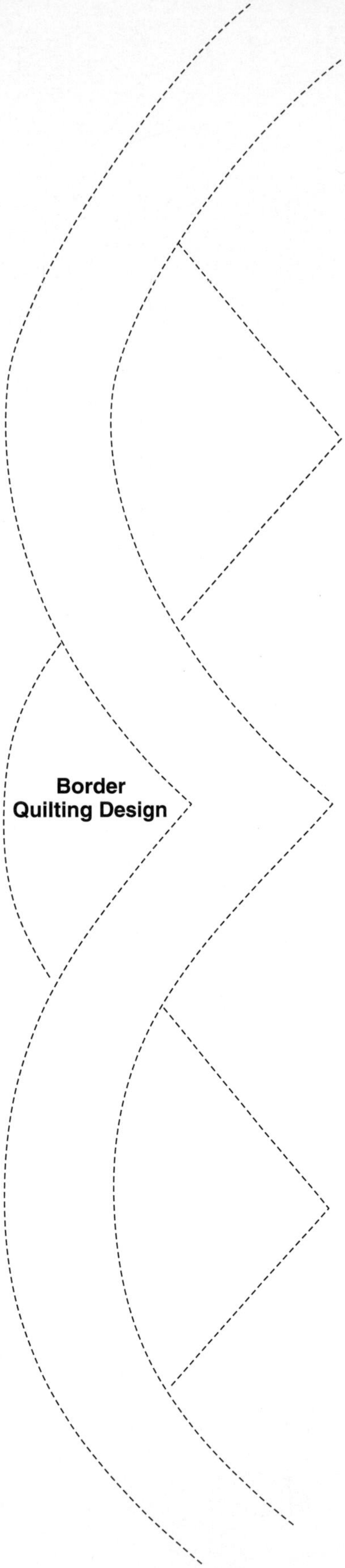

**Border
Quilting Design**

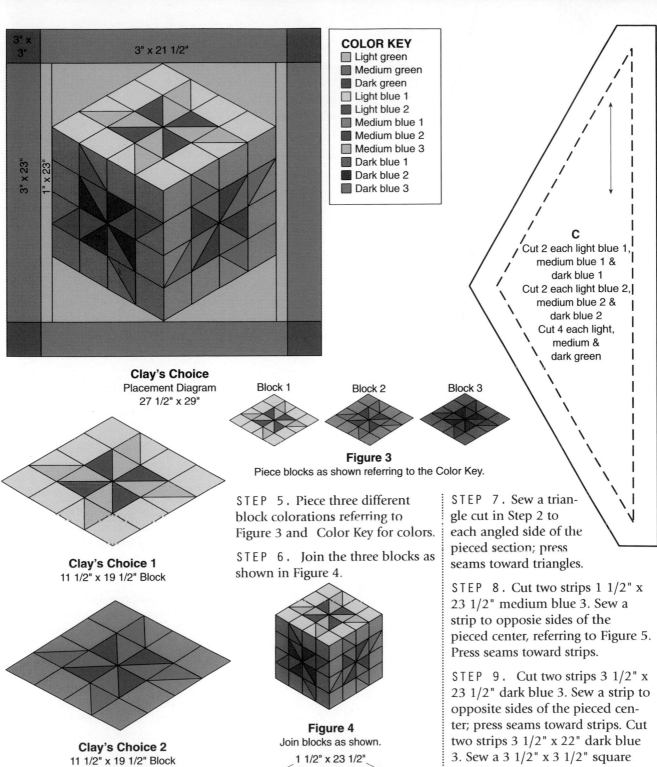

3" x 3"

3" x 21 1/2"

3" x 23"

1" x 23"

COLOR KEY

- ☐ Light green
- ☐ Medium green
- ☐ Dark green
- ☐ Light blue 1
- ☐ Light blue 2
- ☐ Medium blue 1
- ☐ Medium blue 2
- ☐ Medium blue 3
- ☐ Dark blue 1
- ☐ Dark blue 2
- ☐ Dark blue 3

C
Cut 2 each light blue 1,
medium blue 1 &
dark blue 1
Cut 2 each light blue 2,
medium blue 2 &
dark blue 2
Cut 4 each light,
medium &
dark green

Clay's Choice
Placement Diagram
27 1/2" x 29"

Block 1   Block 2   Block 3

Figure 3
Piece blocks as shown referring to the Color Key.

Clay's Choice 1
11 1/2" x 19 1/2" Block

Clay's Choice 2
11 1/2" x 19 1/2" Block

Clay's Choice 3
11 1/2" x 19 1/2" Block

STEP 5. Piece three different block colorations referring to Figure 3 and Color Key for colors.

STEP 6. Join the three blocks as shown in Figure 4.

Figure 4
Join blocks as shown.

1 1/2" x 23 1/2"

Figure 5
Sew a 1 1/2" x 23 1/2" strip to opposite sides.

STEP 7. Sew a triangle cut in Step 2 to each angled side of the pieced section; press seams toward triangles.

STEP 8. Cut two strips 1 1/2" x 23 1/2" medium blue 3. Sew a strip to opposie sides of the pieced center, referring to Figure 5. Press seams toward strips.

STEP 9. Cut two strips 3 1/2" x 23 1/2" dark blue 3. Sew a strip to opposite sides of the pieced center; press seams toward strips. Cut two strips 3 1/2" x 22" dark blue 3. Sew a 3 1/2" x 3 1/2" square cut in Step 3 to each end of each strip. Sew a strip to remaining sides; press seams toward strips.

STEP 10. Prepare quilt for quilting as in General Instructions, using blue metallic thread for quilting. Bind using self-made or purchased binding and finish as directed in General Instructions. ■

By Lucy A. Fazely

Buckeye Beauty

Use fat quarters in any number of colors to create this festive quilt, similar to the Log Cabin Barn-raising design.

INTERMEDIATE SKILL

SPECIFICATIONS
Quilt Size: 48" x 58" (68" x 88" or 88" x 108")

Block Size: 5" x 5"

Number of Blocks: 28 (64 or 108)

MATERIALS
☐ 6 (14 or 22) fat quarters white prints

☐ 6 (14 or 22) fat quarters colored prints

☐ 1 1/4 (1 3/4 or 2 1/4) yards border and binding fabric

☐ Backing 52" x 62" (72" x 92" or 94" x 114")

☐ Batting 52" x 62" (72" x 92" or 94" x 114")

☐ Coordinating all-purpose thread

☐ Basic sewing supplies and tools

PROJECT NOTES
Instructions are given to make three sizes of this quilt. The amounts listed in parentheses in the Project Specifications, list of Materials and in the Instructions are for the alternate sizes. Quilt in photo is 68" x 88".

If you choose to use a different number of fabrics than listed, remember to purchase the same total yardage. For example, if you use 20 fabrics instead of 12, you still need a total of 1 1/2 (3 1/2 or 5 1/2) yards of colored fabrics to complete the quilt.

INSTRUCTIONS
Note: From each fat quarter it is possible to cut either one strip 5 7/8" x 22" and three strips 3" x 22" or two strips 5 7/8" x 22" and one strip 3" x 22". It doesn't matter which choice you make for each fat quarter as long as you have the right total number of colored and white strips as listed.

STEP 1. From both the white and colored fat quarters cut nine (22 or 36) strips 5 7/8" x 22" and 10 (22 or 36) strips 3" x 22". *Note: Extra 3"-wide strips are cut to result in a more random color placement in the quilt.*

STEP 2. Cut 5 7/8" strips into 5 7/8" segments to make squares; you will need 26 (64 or 106) squares each white and colored.

STEP 3. Mark a diagonal line from corner to

corner on the wrong side of each white square. Draw a line 1/4" on each side of the first line as shown in Figure 1.

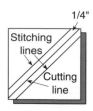

Figure 1
Draw a line 1/4" away from diagonal line on both sides.

STEP 4. Place each white square right sides together with a colored square. Stitch on both 1/4" lines as shown in Figure 2. Repeat for all 5 7/8" x 5 7/8" squares.

Figure 2
Stitch on marked 1/4" lines.

STEP 5. Cut each stitched square along diagonal line; trim excess seam at corners as shown in Figure 3. Open stitched unit to reveal a triangle/square as shown in Figure 4. Press seams toward colored triangle.

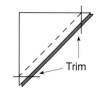

Figure 3
Trim excess at corners.

Figure 4
Open to reveal a triangle/square.

Buckeye Beauty
Placement Diagram
48" x 58"
(68" x 88" & 88" x 108")

STEP 6. Join a 3" x 22" white strip with a 3" x 22" colored strip along 22" side; press seams toward colored strip. Repeat for 10 (22 or 36) strip sets. Cut each strip set into 3" segments. Randomly choose 56 (128 or 216) segments for use in the blocks.

STEP 7. Join two segments to make a Four-Patch block as shown

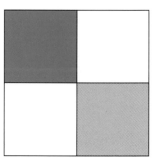

Four-Patch
5" x 5" Block

in Figure 5; press seams in one direction. Repeat for 28 (64 or 108) Four-Patch blocks.

STEP 8. On a flat surface, lay out all triangle/squares with Four-Patch blocks referring to the Placement Diagram for arrangement of blocks. *Note: The darker black lines on the Placement Diagram separate the different sizes of quilts. The inside dark line indicates the 48" x 58" quilt, the next dark line indicates the 68" x 88" quilt, and the largest outside line indicates the 88" x 108" quilt.*

Figure 5
Join 2 segments to make a Four-Patch block.

STEP 9. Join blocks together in rows; press. Join rows together to complete pieced center; press.

STEP 10. Cut six (eight or 10) strips 4 1/2" x 44" for borders. Cut and join strips on short ends to make two strips 50 1/2" (80 1/2" or 100 1/2") and two strips 48 1/2" (68 1/2" or 88 1/2").

STEP 11. Sew the longer strips to opposite long sides of the pieced center and the shorter strips to the top and bottom; press seams toward strips.

STEP 12. Prepare 6 (9 or 11) yards self-made binding using border fabric and referring to the General Instructions.

STEP 13. Prepare quilt for quilting and finish as in General Instructions, binding edges with self-made or purchased binding. ■

By Charlyne Stewart

Garden Path

The traditional Mohawk Trail pattern
has been changed to create a Garden Path
with bright-colored stepping-stones.

INSTRUCTIONS

STEP 1. Make templates for each shape using patterns for Blocks 1, 2 and A. Add seam allowance to each template before cutting. Mark templates with suggested color and number to cut per block as directed on pattern. Cut all pieces as directed.

STEP 2. Piece each block referring to numbers on templates for order of piecing. For Blocks 1 and 2, join pieces 1, 2 and 3; add 4. Join pieces 5, 6 and 7; sew to previously pieced unit; press. Repeat for eight each of Blocks 1 and 2.

STEP 3. Sew the pieced units to piece A, carefully pinning from the center to outside edges as shown in Figure 1. Repeat for all pieced units to complete 16 blocks.

Figure 1
Pin pieced unit to A as shown.

STEP 4. Lay out blocks in four rows of four blocks each referring to Figure 2. Join blocks in rows; join rows. Press seams in one direction.

INTERMEDIATE SKILL

SPECIFICATIONS

Quilt Size: 36" x 36"

Block Size: 8" x 8"

Number of Blocks: 16

MATERIALS

☐ 3/8 yard each red, blue, green, orange, magenta and purple solids

☐ 3/4 yard mottled lime green

☐ 1 yard black solid

☐ Backing 40" x 40"

☐ Batting 40" x 40"

☐ 4 1/2 yards self-made or purchased binding

☐ Coordinating all-purpose thread

☐ 1 spool kelly green quilting thread

☐ Basic sewing supplies

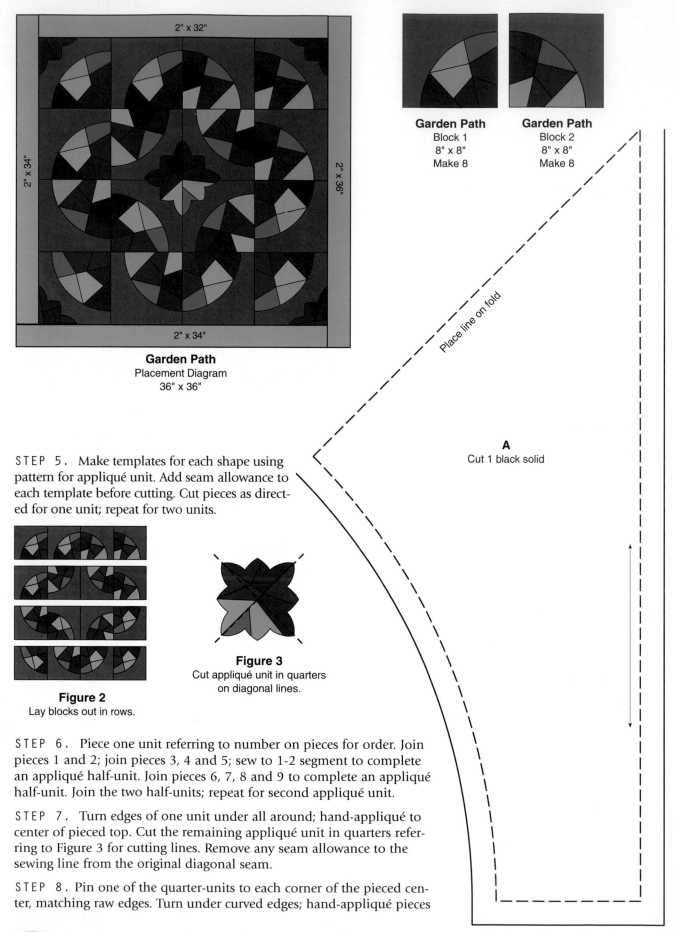

Garden Path
Block 1
8" x 8"
Make 8

Garden Path
Block 2
8" x 8"
Make 8

Garden Path
Placement Diagram
36" x 36"

2" x 32"

2" x 34"

2" x 36"

2" x 34"

Place line on fold

A
Cut 1 black solid

STEP 5. Make templates for each shape using pattern for appliqué unit. Add seam allowance to each template before cutting. Cut pieces as directed for one unit; repeat for two units.

Figure 2
Lay blocks out in rows.

Figure 3
Cut appliqué unit in quarters on diagonal lines.

STEP 6. Piece one unit referring to number on pieces for order. Join pieces 1 and 2; join pieces 3, 4 and 5; sew to 1-2 segment to complete an appliqué half-unit. Join pieces 6, 7, 8 and 9 to complete an appliqué half-unit. Join the two half-units; repeat for second appliqué unit.

STEP 7. Turn edges of one unit under all around; hand-appliqué to center of pieced top. Cut the remaining appliqué unit in quarters referring to Figure 3 for cutting lines. Remove any seam allowance to the sewing line from the original diagonal seam.

STEP 8. Pin one of the quarter-units to each corner of the pieced center, matching raw edges. Turn under curved edges; hand-appliqué pieces

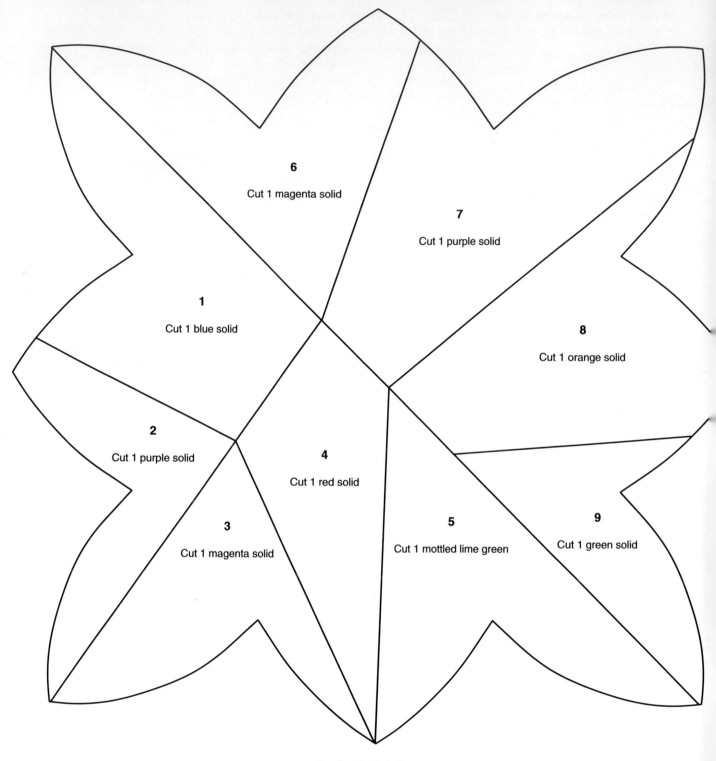

6
Cut 1 magenta solid

7
Cut 1 purple solid

1
Cut 1 blue solid

8
Cut 1 orange solid

2
Cut 1 purple solid

4
Cut 1 red solid

3
Cut 1 magenta solid

5
Cut 1 mottled lime green

9
Cut 1 green solid

Appliqué Unit Pattern
Add 1/4" seam allowance to each template.

in place using matching thread. *Note: Change thread for each different color piece.*

STEP 9. Cut one strip each 2 1/2" x 32 1/2" and 2 1/2" x 36 1/2" and two strips 2 1/2" x 34 1/2" mottled lime green. Sew the shortest strip to top side and longer strips to remaining sides of pieced center referring to the Placement Diagram for order of piecing; press seams toward strips.

STEP 10. Prepare quilt for quilting and finish as in General Instructions, binding edges with self-made or purchased binding. Quilt shown was hand-quilted in the ditch of seams and around appliqué shapes. ■

7
Cut 1 green solid for Block 1
Cut 1 purple solid reversed for Block 2

3
Cut 1 orange solid for Block 1
Cut 1 green solid reversed for Block 2

6
Cut 1 red solid for Block 1
Cut 1 blue solid reversed for Block 2

2
Cut 1 mottled lime green for Block 1
Cut 1 magenta solid reversed for Block 2

5
Cut 1 magenta solid for Block 1
Cut 1 mottled lime green reversed for Block 2

4
Cut 1 blue solid for Block 1
Cut 1 orange solid reversed for Block 2

1
Cut 1 purple solid for Block 1
Cut 1 red solid reversed for Block 2

Block 1 Pattern
Block 2 Pattern Reversed
Add 1/4" seam allowance to each template.

By Connie Rand

Four-Patch Diamonds

Combine several shades of blue to create this monochromatic quilt. Change the color to make an autumn or Christmas version.

INTERMEDIATE SKILL

SPECIFICATIONS

Quilt Size: 55" x 71"

Block Size: 12" x 16"

Number of Blocks: 16

MATERIALS

☐ 2/3 yard medium blue print (blue print 5)

☐ 7/8 yard light medium blue print (blue print 2)

☐ 1 1/8 yards navy solid

☐ 1 1/8 yards lightest blue print (blue print 1)

☐ 1 1/4 yards dark medium blue print (blue print 3)

☐ 2 yards darkest blue print for blocks and borders (blue print 4)

☐ Batting 60" x 76"

☐ Backing 60" x 76"

☐ 7 1/2 yards self-made or purchased binding

☐ Coordinating all-purpose thread

☐ Basic sewing supplies and tools, rotary cutter, ruler and cutting mat

PROJECT NOTE

Gradations of blue are featured in this quilt, but if you prefer, use shades of your favorite color instead.

INSTRUCTIONS

STEP 1. Cut two strips 4" x 48 1/2" and two strips 4" x 64 1/2" blue print 4 from fabric length for borders; set aside.

STEP 2. Prepare templates using pattern pieces given. Cut as directed on each piece for one block; repeat for 16 blocks.

STEP 3. Join four G pieces to make a Four-Patch unit in colors shown in Figure 1.

Figure 1
Sew G pieces together as shown to make a Four-Patch unit.

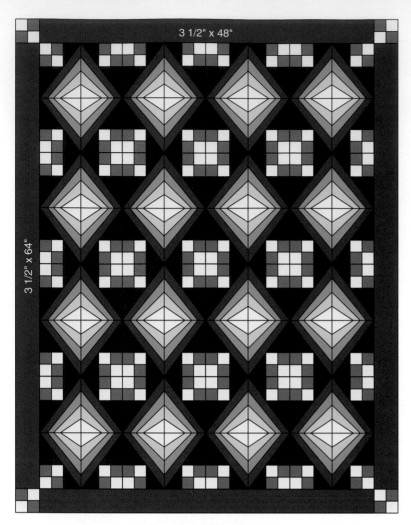

3 1/2" x 48"

3 1/2" x 64"

Four-Patch Diamonds
Placement Diagram
55" x 71"

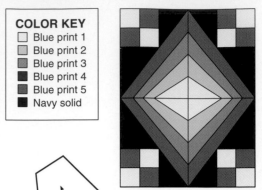

Four-Patch Diamonds
12" x 16" Block

C
Cut 4 blue print 3
(reverse half for CR)

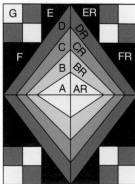

Figure 2
Sew E and F to the
pieced Four-Patch unit.

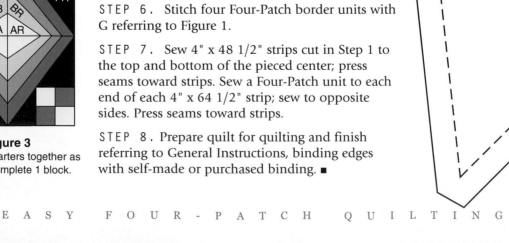

Figure 3
Sew block quarters together as
shown to complete 1 block.

STEP 4. Sew A to B to C to D. Sew E to the previously pieced Four-Patch unit, referring to Figure 2; add F. Sew the E-F-G unit to A-B-C-D to complete one quarter of the block; repeat for two sections. Sew reverse pieces together in same sequence, repeating for two sections. Assemble the block referring to Figure 3; press. Repeat for 16 blocks.

STEP 5. Sew blocks together in four rows of four blocks each to complete quilt center. Press seams in one direction.

STEP 6. Stitch four Four-Patch border units with G referring to Figure 1.

STEP 7. Sew 4" x 48 1/2" strips cut in Step 1 to the top and bottom of the pieced center; press seams toward strips. Sew a Four-Patch unit to each end of each 4" x 64 1/2" strip; sew to opposite sides. Press seams toward strips.

STEP 8. Prepare quilt for quilting and finish referring to General Instructions, binding edges with self-made or purchased binding. ■

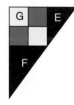

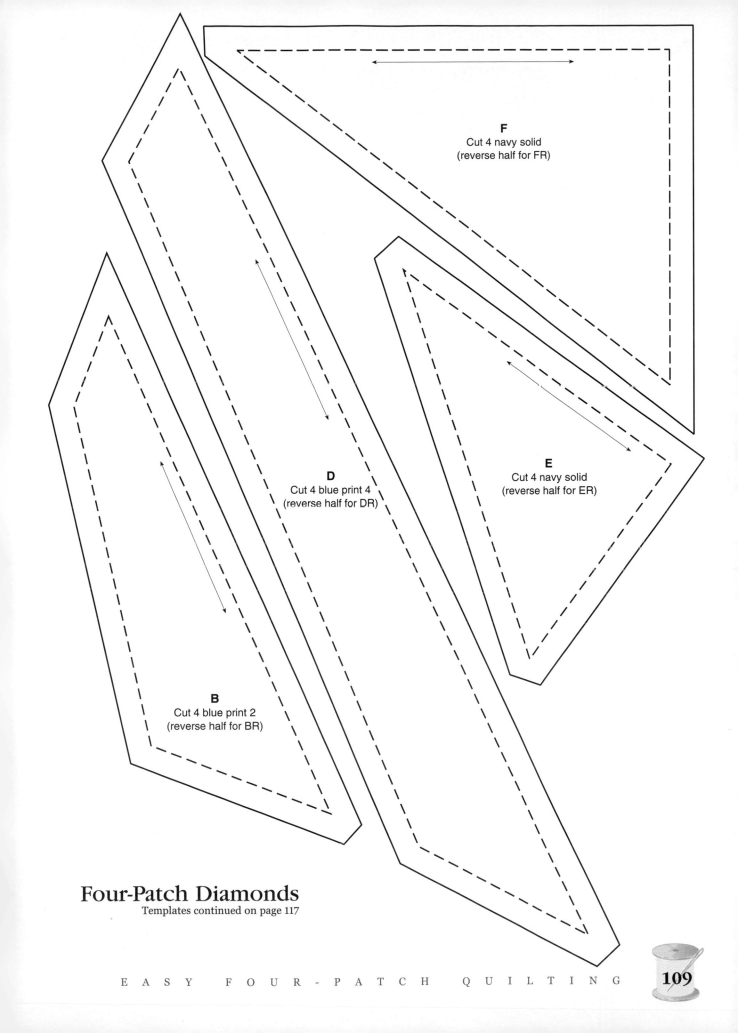

F
Cut 4 navy solid
(reverse half for FR)

D
Cut 4 blue print 4
(reverse half for DR)

E
Cut 4 navy solid
(reverse half for ER)

B
Cut 4 blue print 2
(reverse half for BR)

Four-Patch Diamonds
Templates continued on page 117

By Connie Rand

Four-Patch in the Middle

Make this pattern in patriotic colors and prints to add an accent to your home for the Fourth of July.

INTERMEDIATE SKILL

SPECIFICATIONS
Quilt Size: 30" x 30"

Block Size: 12" x 12"

Number of Blocks: 4

MATERIALS
☐ 1/4 yard patriotic stripe

☐ 3/8 yard red star print

☐ 1/2 yard royal blue solid

☐ 1/2 yard muslin

☐ 1/2 yard coordinating red print for borders

☐ Backing 34" x 34"

☐ Batting 34" x 34"

☐ 4 yards self-made or purchased binding

☐ Coordinating all-purpose thread

☐ Basic sewing supplies and tools

INSTRUCTIONS

STEP 1. Prepare templates for pattern pieces given. Cut as directed on each piece for one block; repeat for four blocks.

STEP 2. To piece one block, sew muslin C and CR to red star B as shown in Figure 1; repeat for four units. Sew blue C to stripe C; repeat for four units. Sew a C-C unit to opposite sides of two B-C units as shown in Figure 2. Sew blue B to blue B and add stripe C to each side; repeat for two units and two units reversed as shown in Figure 3.

Figure 1
Sew C and CR to B;
repeat for 4 units.

Figure 2
Sew C to C; repeat with
CR. Sew to opposite
sides of a B-C unit.

Make 2   Make 2

Figure 3
Sew B to B; add C;
repeat for 2 units and 2 units reversed.

STEP 3. Sew a red star A to a stripe A; repeat for eight units. Join two units to make a Four-Patch

Four-Patch in the Middle
Placement Diagram
30" x 30"

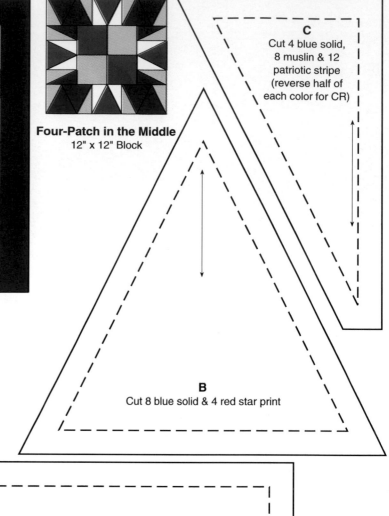

Four-Patch in the Middle
12" x 12" Block

C
Cut 4 blue solid,
8 muslin & 12
patriotic stripe
(reverse half of
each color for CR)

B
Cut 8 blue solid & 4 red star print

A
Cut 2 each red star print & patriotic stripe

unit as shown in Figure 4; repeat for four Four-Patch units.

Figure 4
Join 2 A-A units to make
a Four-Patch unit.

STEP 4. Arrange the pieced units as shown in Figure 5. Join pieced units in rows; join rows to complete one block. Press and repeat for four blocks.

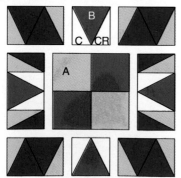

Figure 5
Arrange pieced units in rows;
join to complete 1 block.

STEP 5. Join two blocks to make a row; repeat. Join the rows to complete pieced center; press seams in one direction.

STEP 6. Cut two strips each red border print 3 1/2" x 24 1/2" and 3 1/2" x 30 1/2". Sew the shorter strips to top and bottom and longer strips to opposite sides to complete pieced top. Press seams

toward strips.

STEP 7. Prepare quilt for quilting and finish as in General Instructions, binding edges with self-made or purchased binding. ∎

By Marian Shenk

Star Flower

Use narrow bias strips to create petals around the star shapes to make this pleasing wall quilt.

INSTRUCTIONS

STEP 1. Prepare templates using pattern pieces given. Cut as directed on each piece.

STEP 2. Sew H to HR, stopping and starting at seam allowance as shown in Figure 1.

STEP 3. Cut 1 1/2"-wide bias strips from 16" x 16" square pastel print. Join strips on short ends to make a 5 1/2-yard length of bias. Cut into 16 pieces 10" long. Fold each in half.

STEP 4. Pin raw edge on dotted line marked on H pattern; hand-stitch 1/4" from edge through folded bias tape and H pieces as shown in Figure 2. After stitching, fold bias tape over raw edge to cover seam; hand-stitch in place on folded edge. Repeat for all H-HR units.

Figure 1
Sew H to HR, stopping and starting on seam line as shown.

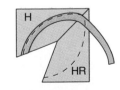

Figure 2
Place raw edge on dotted line; stitch 1/4" away.

STEP 5. Set piece G into H-HR units. Join four H-HR-G units as shown in Figure 3 to make a Star block; press. Repeat for four Star blocks.

STEP 6. Sew A to B to C to D to E; repeat with reverse pieces. Press seams in one direction. Join

ADVANCED SKILL

SPECIFICATIONS

Quilt Size: 26 3/4" x 26 3/4"

Block Size: 8" x 8"

Number of Blocks: 4

MATERIALS

☐ 1/4 yard dark green print for stars and corners

☐ 1/4 yard each green, gold and rose prints for corners

☐ 1/2 yard off-white print for background

☐ 1/2 yard pastel print for corners and bias

☐ 1 yard border stripe

☐ Batting 31" x 31"

☐ Backing 31" x 31"

☐ 3 1/2 yards self-made or purchased binding

☐ Coordinating all-purpose thread

☐ 1 spool off-white quilting thread

☐ Basic sewing supplies and tools

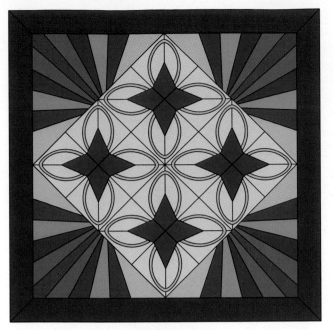

Star Flower
Placement Diagram
26 3/4" x 26 3/4"

Star
8" x 8" Block

two pieced units with F to complete one corner unit as shown in Figure 4; repeat for four corner units.

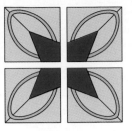

Figure 3
Join 4 units to
make Star block.

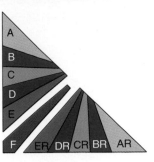

Figure 4
Join pieced units with F.

STEP 7. Sew the four Star blocks together in two rows of two blocks each; join rows to complete center unit. Press seams in one direction.

STEP 8. Sew a corner unit to each side of the center unit; press seams toward corner units.

STEP 9. Cut four strips border print 2 1/2" x 28" (strips are cut longer than needed for mitering), cutting each strip from the same design on border print to make four strips exactly alike. Fold strips crosswise to mark center. Match center of strip to center of pieced quilt top; pin in place. Stitch, mitering corners; press seams toward strips.

STEP 10. Prepare quilt for quilting and finish referring to General Instructions, binding edges with self-made or purchased bias binding. ∎

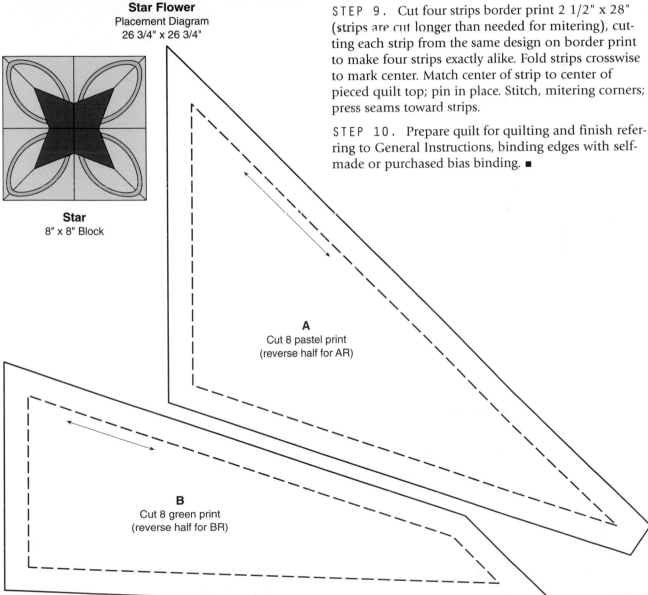

A
Cut 8 pastel print
(reverse half for AR)

B
Cut 8 green print
(reverse half for BR)

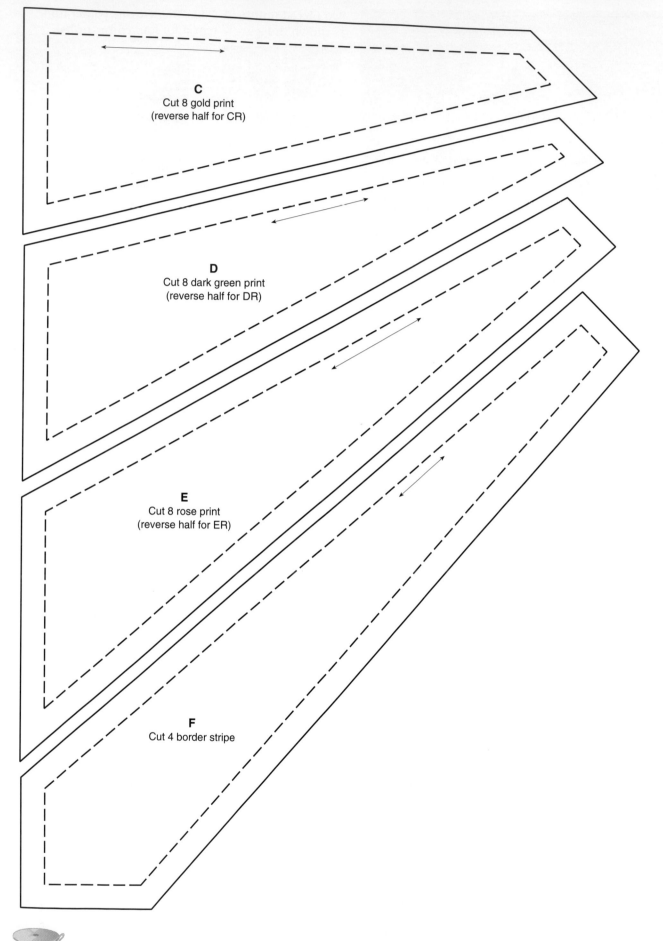

C
Cut 8 gold print
(reverse half for CR)

D
Cut 8 dark green print
(reverse half for DR)

E
Cut 8 rose print
(reverse half for ER)

F
Cut 4 border stripe

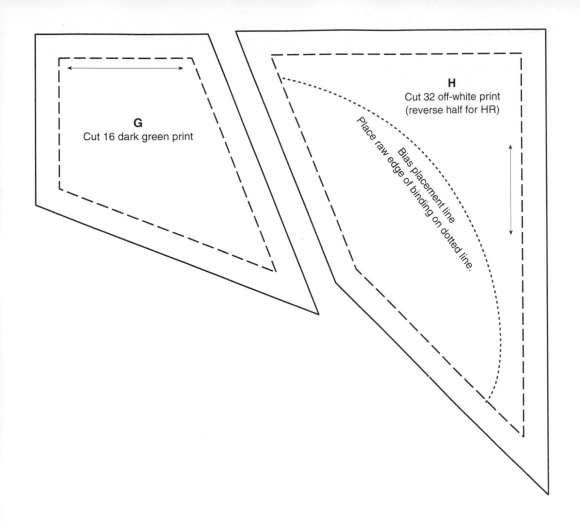

G
Cut 16 dark green print

H
Cut 32 off-white print
(reverse half for HR)

Bias placement line

Place raw edge of binding on dotted line.

Four-Patch Diamonds
Continued from page 109

G
Cut 8 each
blue prints 1 & 5 for block
Cut 2 each blue prints 1 & 5
for border unit

A
Cut 4 blue print 1
(reverse half for AR)

By Jill Reber

Sunny Lanes

Make this bright and cheerful quilt as a baby gift for either a boy or a girl.

INTERMEDIATE SKILL

SPECIFICATIONS
Quilt Size: 47" x 59"

Block Size: 12" x 12"

Number of Blocks: 12

MATERIALS
- ☐ 3/4 yard mottled yellow
- ☐ 3/4 yard mottled blue
- ☐ 1 1/2 yards white solid
- ☐ 3/4 yard yellow plaid
- ☐ Batting 51" x 63"
- ☐ Backing 51" x 63"
- ☐ 6 1/4 yards self-made or purchased binding
- ☐ Coordinating all-purpose thread
- ☐ Basic sewing supplies and tools

INSTRUCTIONS
STEP 1. From white solid cut five strips 3 7/8" by fabric width and 10 strips 2" by fabric width. Cut all 3 7/8" strips into 3 7/8" segments; you will need 48 segments. Cut each segment in half

on one diagonal to make triangles; you will need 96 triangles.

STEP 2. From mottled yellow cut 10 strips 2" by fabric width.

STEP 3. From mottled blue cut five strips 3 7/8" by fabric width; subcut into 3 7/8" segments; you will need 48 segments. Cut each segment in half on one diagonal to make triangles; you will need 96 triangles.

STEP 4. Sew the white solid triangles to the mottled blue triangles to make triangle/squares; repeat for 96 units.

STEP 5. Sew one each 2"-wide white solid and mottled yellow strips together along length; press seams toward mottled yellow. Repeat with all 2" white solid and mottled yellow strips. Subcut into 2" segments; you will need 192 segments.

STEP 6. Join two 2" segments to make a Four-Patch unit as shown in Figure 1; repeat for 96 units.

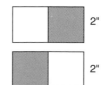

Figure 1
Join two 2" segments to
make a Four-Patch unit.

Sunny Lanes
Placement Diagram
47" x 59"

Sunny Lanes
12" x 12" Block

complete pieced top. Press seams in one direction.

STEP 11. Cut two strips each white solid 2" x 36 1/2" and 2" x 51 1/2". Sew the shorter strips to the top and bottom and longer strips to opposite sides; press seams toward strips.

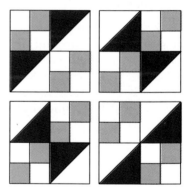

Figure 4
Join units to
complete 1 block.

STEP 12. Cut two strips each yellow plaid 4 1/2" x 39 1/2" and 4 1/2" x 59 1/2". Sew the shorter strips to the top and bottom and longer strips to opposite sides; press seams toward strips.

STEP 13. Prepare quilt for quilting and finish referring to General Instructions, binding edges with self-made or purchased bias binding. ■

STEP 7. Join two Four-Patch units with two triangle/squares to make a block unit as shown in Figure 2; repeat for 24 units.

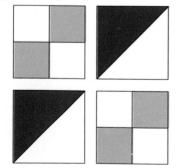

Figure 2
Join 2 Four-Patch units
with 2 triangle/squares.

STEP 8. Join two Four-Patch units with two triangle/squares to make a block unit as shown in Figure 3; repeat for 24 units.

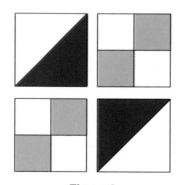

Figure 3
Join 2 Four-Patch units
with 2 triangle/squares.

STEP 9. Join two units made in Step 7 with two units made in Step 8 to make a block as shown in Figure 4.

STEP 10. Arrange blocks in four rows of three blocks each. Join blocks in rows; join rows to

By Ruth M. Swasey

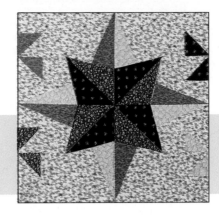

Starry Night

Almost any color matches this tablecloth with its bright yellow and green combined with dark blue and red. Use it on your table to add color to any kitchen or dining area.

INSTRUCTIONS

STEP 1. Prepare templates A and B using pattern pieces given for Pinwheel blocks. Cut as directed on each piece.

STEP 2. To piece one Pinwheel block, sew a white print B to a color print B as shown in Figure 1; repeat for four B-B units. Join each unit with A. Join the four units to complete one block as shown in Figure 2; repeat for eight blocks each in red, navy, green and yellow prints. Press and square up blocks to 6 1/2" x 6 1/2", if necessary.

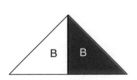

Figure 1
Sew B to B as shown.

Figure 2
Join 4 units to complete
1 Pinwheel block.

STEP 3. Prepare templates C, D and E using pattern pieces given for Blazing Star blocks. Cut as directed on each piece.

STEP 4. To piece one block, sew C to D and add E; repeat for reverse pieces, referring to Figure 3 for color placement. Join these two units to make one-quarter of the block; repeat for four quarters. Join as shown in Figure 4 to complete one block; repeat for 12 blocks. Press and square up blocks to 12 1/2" x 12 1/2", if necessary.

INTERMEDIATE SKILL

SPECIFICATIONS

Quilt Size: 86" x 86"

Block Size: 6" x 6" and
    12" x 12"

Number of Blocks: 32 small
    and 12 large

MATERIALS

☐ 1 1/3 yards each yellow
    and navy prints

☐ 2 1/4 yards each red
    and green prints

☐ 6 1/8 yards white print

☐ 10 yards self-made or
    purchased binding

☐ Neutral color
    all-purpose thread

☐ Basic sewing supplies
    and tools and water-
    erasable marker

STEP 5. Piece one half-block as shown in Figure 5; repeat for eight half-blocks.

STEP 6. Prepare templates for

F and G setting units using pattern pieces given. Cut as directed on each piece.

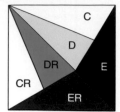

Figure 3
Sew C to D; add E; repeat for CR, DR and ER.

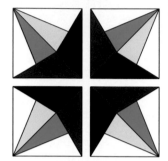

Figure 4
Join units as shown to complete 1 Blazing Star block.

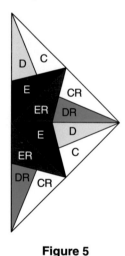

Figure 5
Piece a half-block as shown.

STEP 7. Join two F white print squares with two Pinwheel blocks as shown in Figure 6; repeat for

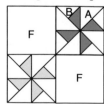

Figure 6
Join 2 F squares with 2 Pinwheel blocks as shown.

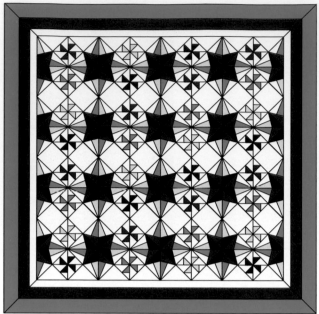

Starry Night Tablecloth
Placement Diagram
86" x 86"

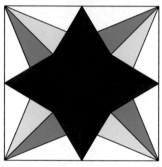

Blazing Star
12" x 12" Block

Pinwheel
6" x 6" Block

12 blocks. Press and square up to 12 1/2" x 12 1/2", if necessary.

STEP 8. Sew two white print G triangles to a Pinwheel block as shown in Figure 7; repeat for eight blocks.

Figure 7
Sew 2 G triangles to a Pinwheel block.

STEP 9. Arrange the blocks and pieced units in diagonal rows as shown in Figure 8. Join blocks in rows; join rows to complete pieced center. Press seams in one direction.

STEP 10. Cut four strips each white print 2 1/2" x 88", red print 3 1/2" x 88" and green print 4 1/2" x 88". Sew a white print strip to a red print strip to a green print strip along length; press seams toward darker fabrics. Repeat for four strips sets. *Note: Strips are cut 1 1/2" longer than needed; excess will be trimmed after mitering.*

STEP 11. Fold strips to find center; pin. Fold pieced top to find center; pin. Pin border strips to quilt sides with white strip toward inside, matching centers. Stitch strips to sides, mitering corners referring to General Instructions. *Note: The sample has no batting or backing but has bound edges. If you prefer to finish with batting and backing, purchase backing fabric to make a backing 90" x 90" and a batting the same size. Refer to General Instructions for finishing with backing and batting.*

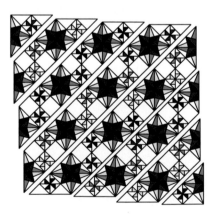

Figure 8
Arrange blocks and pieced units in diagonal rows.

STEP 12. Press entire top. Bind edges referring to General Instructions to finish. ■

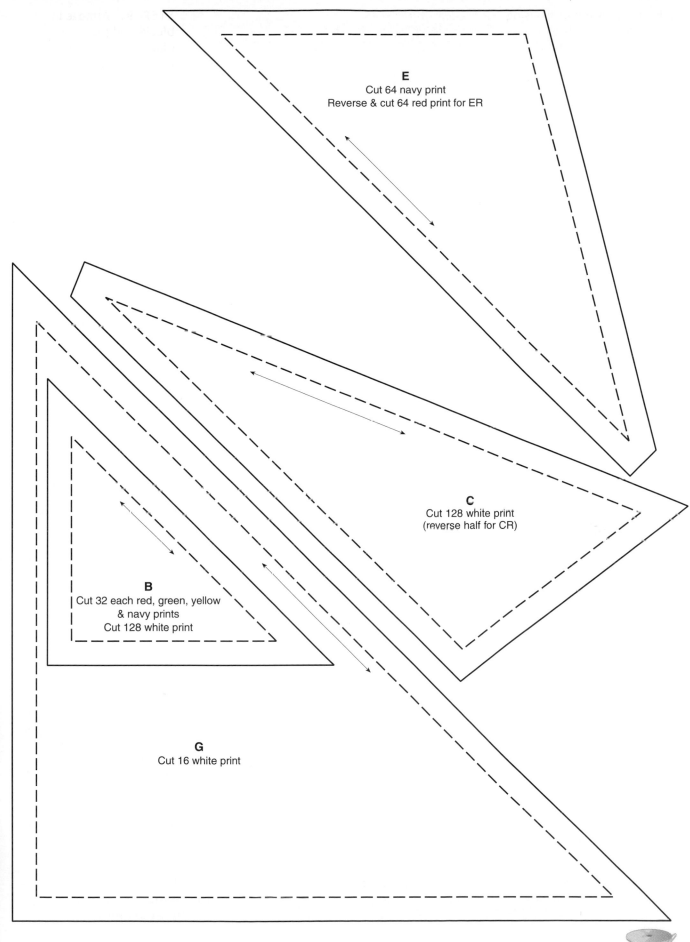

E
Cut 64 navy print
Reverse & cut 64 red print for ER

C
Cut 128 white print
(reverse half for CR)

B
Cut 32 each red, green, yellow
& navy prints
Cut 128 white print

G
Cut 16 white print

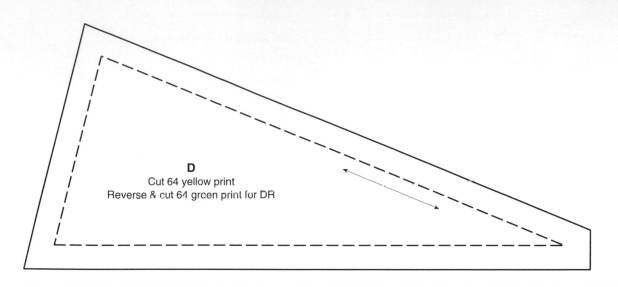

D
Cut 64 yellow print
Reverse & cut 64 green print for DR

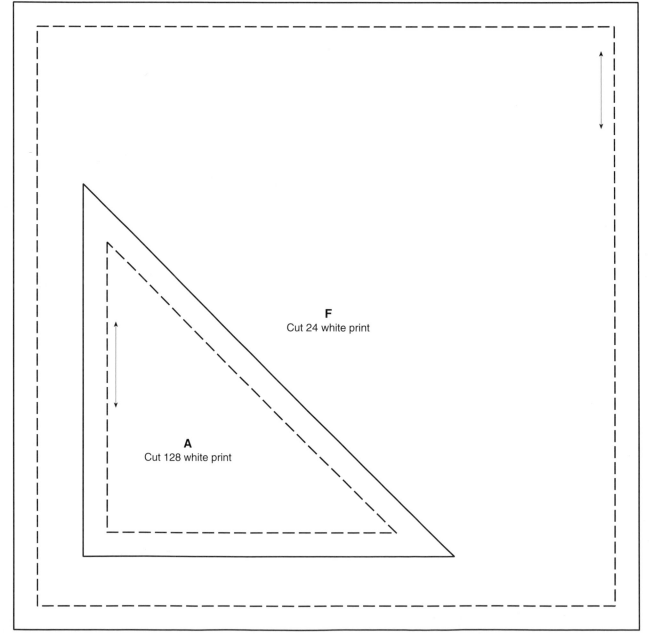

F
Cut 24 white print

A
Cut 128 white print

By Ruth Swasey

Red & White Album

Strawberry prints combine with red and white fabrics to make this summery-looking quilt.

SPECIFICATIONS

Quilt Size: 84" x 92 1/2"

Block Size: 12" x 12"

Number of Blocks: 42

MATERIALS

☐ 3/4 yard each strawberry prints 1, 2 and 3

☐ 3 1/4 yards white solid

☐ 3 yards red print 1 for blocks

☐ 1 yard red print 2 for border

☐ Backing 88" x 97"

☐ Batting 88" x 97"

☐ Neutral color all-purpose thread

☐ Basic sewing supplies and tools

PROJECT NOTES

If you prefer traditional piecing, patterns are given for template shapes. Cut as directed on each piece to make one block.

Red is listed on templates without differentiating between red print and strawberry prints.

INSTRUCTIONS

STEP 1. Cut six strips white solid and 12 strips 2 5/8" by fabric width red print 1. Sew a white strip between two red strips; press seams toward red. Repeat for six strip sets; cut into 2 5/8" segments to make 84 B-B-B units as shown in Figure 1.

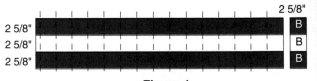

Figure 1
Cut into 2 5/8" segments to make B-B-B units.

STEP 2. Cut seven strips white solid 2 5/8" by fabric width. Cut into 6 7/8" segments for D; you will need 42 white solid D segments.

STEP 3. Cut 20 strips 2 5/8" by fabric width red print 1. Cut into 6 7/8" segments for D; you will need 120 red print 1 D segments.

STEP 4. Cut eight strips 2 5/8" by fabric width red print 1. Cut into 2 5/8" square segments for B; you will need 120 red print 1 B squares.

STEP 5. Cut two strips each 2 5/8" by fabric width strawberry prints 1 and 2. Cut into 2 5/8" square segments for B; you will need 24 each

 3 1/2" x 89"
2 1/2" x 86 1/2"

3 1/2" x 77"
3 1/2" x 84"

Red & White Album Quilt
Placement Diagram
84" x 92 1/2"

Album
12" x 12" Block

STEP 12. Arrange pieced units with two D's as shown in Figure 5; join to complete one block. Press; repeat for 18 red-and-white blocks and 12 strawberry print 1 and 12 strawberry print 2 blocks as shown in Figure 6.

Figure 5
Arrange units as shown;
stitch to complete 1 block.

Red Print 1 Make 18	Strawberry Print 1 Make 12	Strawberry Print 2 Make 12

Figure 6
Make blocks as shown.

strawberry prints 1 and 2 B squares.

STEP 6. Cut four strips each 2 5/8" by fabric width strawberry prints 1 and 2; cut into 6 7/8" segments for D. You will need 24 each strawberry prints 1 and 2 D segments.

STEP 7. Cut four strips white solid 3 3/8" by fabric width. Cut into 3 3/8" square segments; you will need 42 squares. Cut each square on both diagonals to make A triangles. You will need 168 white solid A triangles.

STEP 8. Cut 18 strips white solid 3" by fabric width. Cut into 3" square segments; you will need 252 squares. Cut each square on one diagonal to make C triangles. You will need 504 white solid C triangles.

STEP 9. To piece one block, sew C to opposite sides of a B square as shown in Figure 2; add A. Repeat for four A-B-C units.

STEP 10. Sew C to short sides of

D as shown in Figure 3; repeat for two C-D units.

Figure 2
Sew C pieces to B; add A.

Figure 3
Sew C to D.

STEP 11. Sew a B-B-B unit to opposite long sides of D as shown in Figure 4.

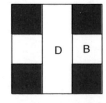

Figure 4
Sew 2 B-B-B units to D.

R	S1	S2	S1	S2	R
R	S2	S1	S2	S1	R
R	S1	S2	S1	S2	R
R	S2	S1	S2	S1	R
R	S1	S2	S1	S2	R
R	S2	S1	S2	S1	R
R	R	R	R	R	R

Figure 7
Arrange blocks as shown.
R = Red print 1
S1 = Strawberry print 1
S2 = Strawberry print 2

STEP 13. Arrange blocks in seven rows of six blocks each, arranging different fabric blocks as shown in Figure 7. Join blocks in rows; join rows to complete pieced center. Press seams in one direction.

STEP 14. Cut and piece two border strips each 3" x 84 1/2" and 3" x 77 1/2" from strawberry print 3. Sew longer strips to opposite long sides and shorter strips to top and bottom of pieced center; press seams toward strips.

STEP 15. Cut and piece two long border strips 4" x 89 1/2" and one strip 4" x 84 1/2" from red print 2. Sew longer strips to opposite long sides and shorter strip to the bottom of pieced center; press seams toward strips. *Note: There is no red print border strip on the top of the quilt shown.*

STEP 16. Prepare top for quilting and finish referring to General Instructions. *Note: Binding for this quilt was made using one each 7"-wide strip white solid and strawberry prints 1 and 2. Join strips along long sides cut into 2"-wide segments. Join on the short ends to make 10 1/2 yards self-made binding.* ■

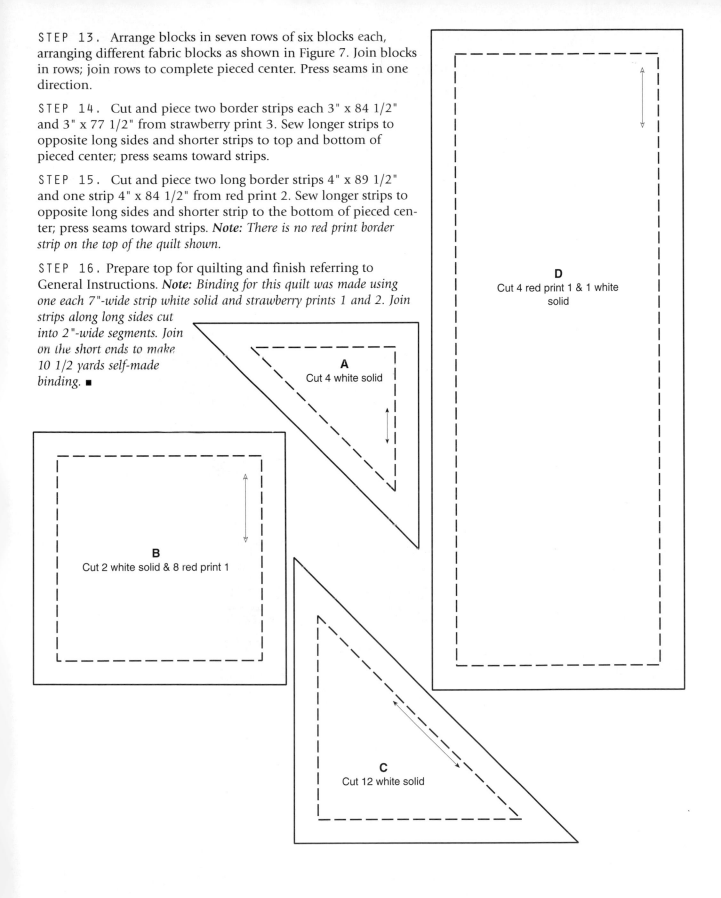

A
Cut 4 white solid

B
Cut 2 white solid & 8 red print 1

C
Cut 12 white solid

D
Cut 4 red print 1 & 1 white solid

By Norma Storm

Puss in the Corner

Cat lovers will enjoy this easy-to-make quilt in primary colors.

INTERMEDIATE SKILL

SPECIFICATIONS
Quilt Size: 44" x 60"

Pillow Size: 16" x 16"

Block Size: 8" x 8"

Number of Blocks: 39

MATERIALS
☐ 1/4 yard each yellow and green solids

☐ 1 yard red solid

☐ 1 yard blue solid

☐ 1 3/4 yards white solid

☐ 19 assorted pieces each 6" x 8" for cats (1 yard if you prefer to use only 1 fabric)

☐ Backing 45" x 61"

☐ Batting 45" x 61"

☐ Batting 17" x 17" for pillow

☐ Backing 17" x 17" for pillow

☐ 16" pillow form

☐ 1 3/4 yards fusible transfer web

☐ 1 3/4 yards fabric stabilizer

☐ 1 spool each white and neutral color all-purpose thread

☐ Basic sewing supplies and tools, rotary cutter, ruler and mat

Quilt
INSTRUCTIONS
STEP 1. Cut six strips blue solid 2 1/2" by fabric width and three strips red solid 4 1/2" by fabric width. Sew a red strip between two blue strips; press seams toward blue. Repeat for three strip sets; cut into 2 1/2" segments as shown in Figure 1. You will need 40 units.

STEP 2. Cut six strips red solid 2 1/2" by fabric width and three strips white solid 4 1/2" by fabric width. Sew a white strip between two red strips; press seams

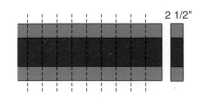

2 1/2"

Figure 1
Cut strip set into 2 1/2" segments.

Puss in the Corner
8" x 8" Block
Make 20

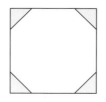

Snowball
8" x 8" Block
Make 19

Puss in the Corner
Placement Diagram
44" x 60"

2" x 44"

2" x 56"

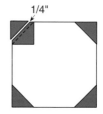

Puss in the Corner Pillow
Placement Diagram

shown in Figure 5 to complete one Snowball block; repeat for nine blocks with green corners and 10 with yellow corners. Set aside one block of each color for pillow.

1/4"

Figure 5
Trim 1/4" from seam; press
to complete 1 Snowball block.

STEP 7. Cut 19 pieces 6" x 8" fusible transfer web. Fuse web to wrong side of each piece cat fabric following manufacturer's instructions; remove paper backing.

STEP 8. Make template for cat using full-size pattern given. Cut as directed on piece.

STEP 9. Center one cat on each yellow Snowball block with nine cats facing right and one facing left; fuse in place. Repeat with each green Snowball block with cats facing left.

STEP 10. Place a piece of fabric stabilizer under each cat. Using white thread, machine-appliqué cats in place, stitching detail lines as marked on pattern at the same time.

STEP 11. Arrange blocks in

toward red. Repeat for three strip sets; cut into 4 1/2" segments as shown in Figure 2. You will need 20 segments.

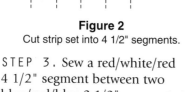

4 1/2"

Figure 2
Cut strip set into 4 1/2" segments.

STEP 3. Sew a red/white/red 4 1/2" segment between two blue/red/blue 2 1/2" segments to complete one Puss in the Corner block as shown in Figure 3. Repeat

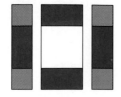

Figure 3
Join segments to complete 1
Puss in the Corner block.

for 20 blocks; set aside two for pillow.

STEP 4. Cut three strips each green and yellow solids 2 1/2" by fabric width. Cut each strip into 2 1/2" square segments. You will need 36 green and 40 yellow squares.

STEP 5. Cut 19 squares white solid 8 1/2" x 8 1/2". Place a 2 1/2" x 2 1/2" green square on each corner of one 8 1/2" x 8 1/2" white square. Sew on one diagonal of each square as shown in Figure 4.

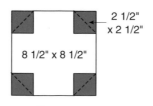

2 1/2"
x 2 1/2"

8 1/2" x 8 1/2"

Figure 4
Sew on 1 diagonal of each square.

STEP 6. Trim excess off 1/4" from stitching line and press as

rows referring to the Placement Diagram for color placement. Join blocks in rows; join rows. Press all seams.

STEP 12. Cut and piece two strips each blue solid 2 1/2" x 44 1/2" and 2 1/2" x 56 1/2". Sew the longer strips to opposite sides and the shorter strips to top and bottom; press seams toward strips.

STEP 13. Place batting on a flat surface. Place backing right side up on batting and pieced top right sides together with backing. Pin or baste layers together. Stitch all around outside edges, leaving a

12" opening on one side. Trim corners and batting and backing.

STEP 14. Turn right side out through opening. Press to flatten edge. Pin layers together. Hand-stitch opening closed.

STEP 15. Machine-quilt all vertical and horizontal seams and diagonal lines through each Puss in the Corner block and around each cat shape.

Pillow
INSTRUCTIONS

STEP 1. Join two Puss in the Corner blocks with two Snowball blocks referring to the Placement

Diagram for positioning.

STEP 2. Place the 17" x 17" piece of batting behind the pieced block section; pin or baste layers together. Quilt as desired by hand or machine. When quilting is complete, trim edges even and remove pins or basting.

STEP 3. Place backing right sides together with quilted block. Stitch around outside edges, leaving one side open. Trim backing even with pillow top; turn right side out.

STEP 4. Insert pillow form through opening. Hand-stitch opening closed to finish. ■

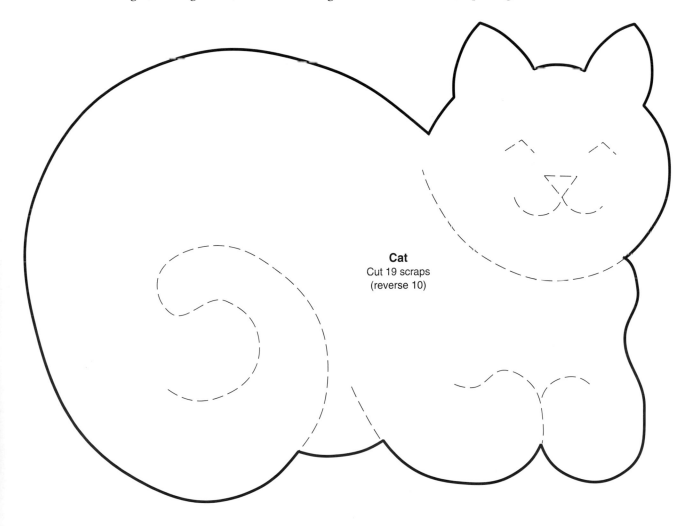

Cat
Cut 19 scraps
(reverse 10)

By Kate Laucomer

Kali's Star

Blue-and-white quilts, star quilts and my 4-year-old daugher Kali—three of my favorite things. The Double Four-Patch inside a Sawtooth Star is a simple pattern made more charming by the star and cable quilting. Make the wall quilt with a table runner to match.

INTERMEDIATE SKILL

SPECIFICATIONS
Quilt Size: 30" x 30"

Block Size: 8" x 8"

Number of Blocks: 9

MATERIALS
☐ 1/4 yard white prints for inner border

☐ 3/8 yard navy prints for outer border

☐ 1/2 yard white prints for blocks

☐ 5/8 yard navy prints for blocks

☐ Backing 34" x 34"

☐ Batting 34" x 34"

☐ 4 yards self-made binding

☐ 1 spool each white and navy all-purpose thread

☐ Basic sewing supplies and tools

PROJECT NOTE
These projects use scraps of different blue and white prints. The yardage given in the Materials lists refers to the total yardage needed of these prints. One fabric or many may be used. After cutting squares from fabrics, I found it easier to put all dark or light squares of one size in different plastic bags. Then I shook them up and chose one square at a time from each bag.

Wall Quilt
INSTRUCTIONS
STEP 1. Cut 36 squares each white and navy prints 1 1/2" x 1 1/2" for A. Cut 54 squares each white and navy prints 2 7/8" x 2 7/8" for B. Cut 18 squares navy prints 2 1/2" x 2 1/2" for C.

STEP 2. Draw a diagonal line on one 2 7/8" x 2 7/8" white print square. Place right sides together with a same-size navy print square; sew 1/4" on each side of the drawn line as shown in Figure 1. Cut apart on drawn line; press triangle/squares seams open. Repeat with all 54 squares to make 108 B triangle/square units.

Figure 1
Sew 1/4" on each side of diagonal line.

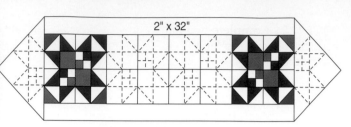

Kali's Star Table Runner
Placement Diagram
12" x 44"

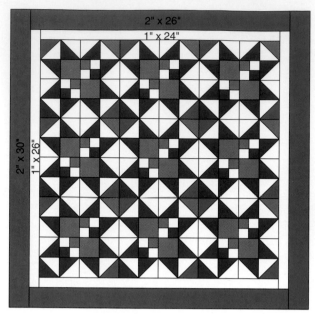

Kali's Star Wall Quilt
Placement Diagram
30" x 30"

Kali's Star
8" x 8" Block

STEP 3. Sew a 1 1/2" x 1 1/2" white print A square to a same-size navy square; press seams toward navy side. Repeat for all A squares. Join two A-A units to make a Four-Patch unit as shown in Figure 2. Repeat with all A squares to make 18 Four-Patch units; press seams open.

Figure 2
Join 2 A-A units to make
a Four-Patch unit.

STEP 4. Arrange A triangle/ squares with B Four-Patch units and C squares to make block quarters as shown in Figure 3; repeat for 18 quarters of each version shown. Join four block quarters to

Figure 3
Join units as shown to
complete block quarters.

complete one block as shown in Figure 4; press seams open.

Figure 4
Join quarters to
complete 1 block.

STEP 5. Arrange blocks in three rows of three blocks each. Join blocks in rows; join rows to complete pieced center. Press seams open.

STEP 6. Cut two strips white print 1 1/2" x 24 1/2" and two strips 1 1/2" x 26 1/2". Sew the shorter strips to top and bottom and longer strips to remaining opposite sides; press seams open.

STEP 7. Cut two strips navy print 2 1/2" x 26 1/2" and two strips 2 1/2" x 30 1/2". Sew the

shorter strips to top and bottom and longer strips to remaining opposite sides; press seams open.

STEP 8. Prepare quilt top for quilting and finishing using self-made binding referring to General Instructions. ***Note:*** *The quilt shown was machine-quilted in the ditch of seams around star points and with a tiny cable design on the borders and into the white triangle/squares at the side edges of the blocks.*

Table Runner

INTERMEDIATE SKILL

SPECIFICATIONS
Table Runner Size: 12" x 44"

Block Size: 8" x 8"

Number of Blocks: 2

MATERIALS

☐ 1/4 yard navy prints for blocks

☐ 3/4 yard white prints for blocks and borders

☐ Backing 16" x 48"

☐ Batting 16" x 48"

☐ 3 1/2 yards self-made binding

☐ 1 spool each white and navy all-purpose thread

☐ Basic sewing supplies and tools

INSTRUCTIONS
STEP 1. Cut eight squares each white and navy prints 1 1/2" x 1 1/2" for A. Cut 12 squares each white and navy prints 2 7/8" x 2 7/8"for B. Cut four squares navy prints 2 1/2" x 2 1/2" for C.

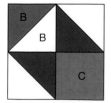

STEP 2. Complete two Kali's Star blocks referring to Steps 2–4 for Wall Quilt.

STEP 3. Cut eight squares light print 4 1/2" x 4 1/2". Join two squares; repeat. Join these two units to complete one large Four-Patch block; repeat for two blocks; press seams open.

STEP 4. Join the two large Four-Patch blocks; sew a Kali's Star block to each end of this pieced unit as shown in Figure 5. Press seams open.

Figure 5
Sew a pieced block to each end of 2-block unit.

STEP 5. Cut two strips white print 2 1/2" x 32 1/2". Sew a strip to opposite long sides of pieced block strip; press seams open.

STEP 6. Cut one square white print 9 3/8" x 9 3/8". Cut the square on one diagonal to make two triangles. Sew a triangle to each end of the pieced section; press seams open.

STEP 7. Mark the two center large Four-Patch blocks with the star block design using pattern given and referring to Figure 6. Mark the two end triangles with half the star block design using same pattern and referring to the Placement Diagram.

STEP 8. Prepare table runner top for quilting and finishing

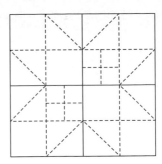

Figure 6
Mark quilting design on large Four-Patch blocks.

using self-made binding referring to General Instructions. *Note: The quilt shown was machine-quilted in the larger Four-Patch blocks and around star design in pieced blocks and machine-quilted with a tiny cable design on the borders and into the white triangle/squares at the side edges of the blocks.* ■

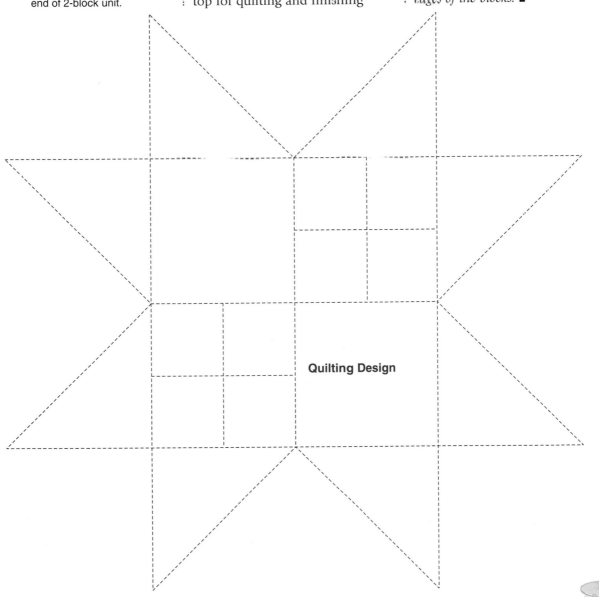

Quilting Design

GRANDMOTHER'S HOPE CHEST

Open up this chapter full of quilts like those Grandmother made, and you'll find treasures you want to stitch and pass down to your children and grandchildren. There are many reproduction fabrics available today that make this a very possible dream come true. Each of these classic designs is based on a traditional Four-Patch quilt, but the variety of colors and settings used gives each quilt a distinct look and charm all its own.

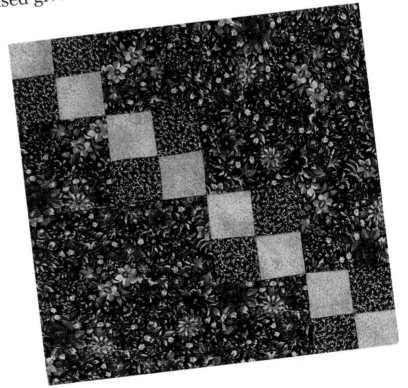

By Nancy Kiman

Scrappy Arrow

Scrap quilts are so much fun to make. The quilt shown was an ongoing project for months as I collected scraps and completed blocks. By the time I finished, I had made enough blocks to make this quilt, a matching pillow and table runner.

INTERMEDIATE SKILL

SPECIFICATIONS

Quilt Size: 94" x 110"

Block Size: 8" x 8"

Number of Blocks: 120

MATERIALS

☐ 1 3/4 yards total medium print scraps

☐ 3 3/4 yards beige print for blocks and borders

☐ 4 1/2 yards total dark print scraps

☐ Backing 98" x 114"

☐ Batting 98" x 114"

☐ 12 yards self-made or purchased binding

☐ Neutral color all-purpose thread

☐ Basic sewing supplies and tools, rotary cutter, ruler and cutting mat

PROJECT NOTE

The objective when making the Arrow Four-Patch blocks is to purchase enough of one light-colored fabric to use in all blocks. Each block uses a dark and medium print combined with the background to be successful. If the background is used on the borders, the quilt has a balanced look even though made with scraps.

Four-Patch Quilt

INSTRUCTIONS

STEP 1. Cut two strips each beige print 7 1/2" x 94 1/2" and 7 1/2" x 96 1/2" from fabric length; set aside for borders.

STEP 2. For one block, cut four squares 2 1/2" x 2 1/2" and two squares 4 1/2" x 4 1/2" dark print and one strip each medium and beige prints 1 1/2" x 12".

STEP 3. Sew the 1 1/2" x 12" medium and beige print strips together along the 12" sides. Press

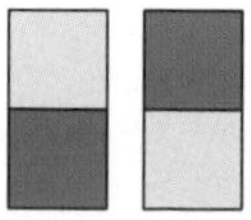

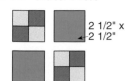

2 1/2" x 2 1/2"

Figure 2
Join two 2 1/2" squares with 2
Four-Patch units to complete
a larger Four-Patch unit.

Figure 1
Join 2 pieced units to
make a Four-Patch unit.

seams toward medium print. Subcut strip set into eight 1 1/2" units. Join two units to make a Four-Patch unit as shown in Figure 1; repeat for four Four-Patch units.

S T E P   4 . Join two 2 1/2" x 2 1/2" squares dark print with two Four-Patch units to make a larger Four-Patch unit as shown in Figure 2; repeat.

S T E P   5 . Join the two larger Four-Patch units with two 4 1/2" x 4 1/2" dark squares to complete one block as shown in Figure 3; press. Repeat for 120 blocks using

4 1/2" x 4 1/2"

Figure 3
Join units as shown
to make 1 block.

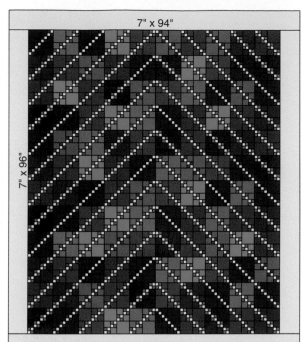

7" x 94"

7" x 96"

7" x 96"

**Scrappy Arrow
Four-Patch**
Placement Diagram
94" x 110"

Arrow Four-Patch
8" x 8" Block

a variety of scrap fabrics with beige print.

S T E P   6 . Arrange blocks in 12 rows of 10 blocks each. Join blocks in rows; join rows to complete pieced center. Press seams in one direction.

S T E P   7 . Sew a 7 1/2" x 96 1/2" beige print strip cut in Step 1 to the opposite long sides of pieced center; press seams toward strips. Sew the 7 1/2" x 94 1/2" beige print strips cut in Step 1 to the top and bottom; press seams toward strips.

S T E P   8 . Prepare quilt top for quilting and finish referring to the General Instructions.

Arrow Four-Patch Pillow

BEGINNER SKILL

S P E C I F I C A T I O N S
Pillow Size: 18" x 18" (without flange)
Block Size: 8" x 8"
Number of Blocks: 4
M A T E R I A L S
☐ 8" x 10" scrap each of 4 dark prints
☐ 1 1/2" x 12" scrap each of 4 medium prints
☐ 3/4 yard beige print
☐ Batting 22" x 22"
☐ Lining 22" x 22"
☐ 18" x 18" pillow form
☐ Neutral color all-purpose thread
☐ Basic sewing supplies and tools, rotary cutter, ruler and cutting mat

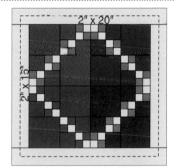

2" x 20"

2" x 18"

Arrow Four-Patch Pillow
Placement Diagram
18" x 18" (without flange)

I N S T R U C T I O N S
S T E P   1 . Complete four Arrow Four-Patch blocks referring to Steps 1–5 for quilt.

S T E P   2 . Lay out blocks on a flat surface referring to Figure 4. Join blocks in rows; join rows to complete pillow top.

Figure 4
Lay out 4 blocks as
shown for pillow top.

S T E P   3 . Cut two strips each beige print 2 1/2" x 16 1/2" and 2 1/2" x 20 1/2". Sew the shorter strips to opposite sides of pieced center; press seams toward strips. Sew the longer strips to the remaining sides; press seams toward center.

S T E P   4 . Sandwich batting square between pillow top and lining piece. Pin or baste layers together. Quilt as desired by hand or machine. When quilting is complete, trim edges even; remove pins or basting.

S T E P   5 . Cut two pieces beige print 15 3/4" x 20 1/2" for backing pieces. Turn under one 15 3/4" edge of each piece 1/4" and 1/4" again for hem; stitch to hold in place (pieces will measure 15 1/4" x 20 1/2").

S T E P   6 . Layer two hemmed pieces right sides up, overlapping one hemmed edge over the other 10" as shown in Figure 5.

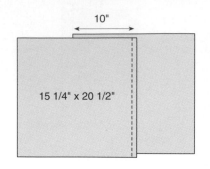

10"

15 1/4" x 20 1/2"

Figure 5
Overlap pieces 10" as shown.

STEP 7. Place pieced top right sides together with hemmed pieces; pin. Sew around outside edges. Clip corners and turn right side out through overlapped opening.

STEP 8. Stitch 1" from outside

edge all around cover to make pillow flange referring to the Placement Diagram.

STEP 9. Slip pillow form through opening on back to finish.

Arrow Four-Patch Table Runner

SPECIFICATIONS

Table Runner Size:
    Approximately 11 1/2" x 64"

Block Size: 8" x 8"

Number of Blocks: 5

MATERIALS

- 8" x 10" scrap each of 5 dark prints
- 1 1/2" x 12" scrap each of 5 medium prints
- 5/8 yard beige print
- Batting 15" x 68"
- Backing 15" x 68"
- 4 1/2 yards self-made binding
- Neutral color all-purpose thread
- Basic sewing supplies and tools, rotary cutter, ruler and cutting mat

INSTRUCTIONS

STEP 1. Complete five Arrow Four-Patch blocks referring to Steps 1–5 for quilt.

STEP 2. Cut two squares beige print 12 5/8" x 12 5/8". Cut each square on both diagonals to make

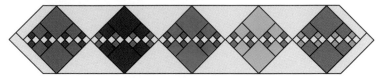

Arrow Four-Patch Table Runner
Placement Diagram
Approximately 11 1/2" x 64"

a total of eight triangles. Cut two strips each beige print 3" x 8 1/2" and 3" x 11" for ends.

STEP 3. Sew a triangle to two opposite sides of a pieced block as shown in Figure 6. Repeat for three units. Sew a triangle to one side of the remaining two blocks; press seams toward triangles.

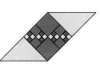

Figure 6
Sew a triangle to opposite sides of a pieced block.

STEP 4. Arrange the pieced units as shown in Figure 7. Join units; press seams in one direction.

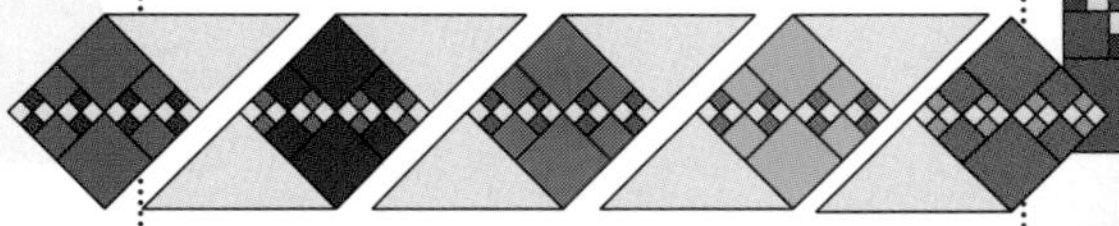

Figure 7
Arrange pieced units as shown.

STEP 5. Sew a 3" x 8 1/2" strip to one side of each end unit and trim even with triangle as shown in Figure 8; press seams toward

strips. Sew a 3" x 11" strip to the adjacent side of end unit; trim even with triangle edge as before.

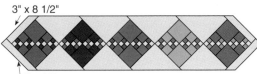

3" x 8 1/2"

3" x 11"

Figure 8
Trim excess strips even with triangles.

STEP 6. Prepare table runner for quilting and finish referring to the General Instructions. ∎

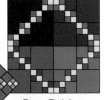

Barn-Raising

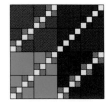

Straight Furrows

Pinwheels

Figure 9
Blocks may be arranged in several designs.

By Sandra L. Hatch

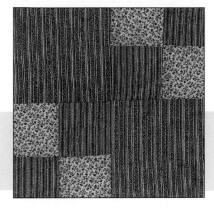

Double Four-Patch

This Double Four-Patch quilt was created using some vintage blocks made with black-and-white shirting prints combined with an unusual mixture of other prints. Make your version in a planned color arrangement from scraps.

PROJECT NOTES

I never noticed until the quilt was finished that I had turned one block in the wrong direction and that two blocks were pieced opposite the others. Look at the photo of the quilt to find these mistakes. Regardless, this quilt looks great on a bed.

I was given a box of old fabrics and blocks that were purchased at a yard sale. These blocks were in the box. I had to plan a quilt in which I could use them all. I had just the right number, except one block was yellow. It stuck out like a sore thumb so I replaced it with a block made using the scraps in the box. The corner blocks were pieced using scraps and the sashing fabric to tie this fabric into the quilt.

INSTRUCTIONS

STEP 1. Cut two strips each black print 3" x 48" and 3" x 73" along length of fabric; set aside for inner borders.

STEP 2. Cut 96 squares dark prints and 123 squares light prints 3" x 3". *Note: If using scraps, you need four squares of the same light and dark fabrics for each block.* Cut eight 3" x 3" squares black print for border Four-Patch units. Set aside 19 squares light print for sashing and eight squares for border Four-Patch units.

STEP 3. Sew a light square to a dark square; repeat. Join the two units to make a Four-Patch

BEGINNER SKILL

SPECIFICATIONS

Quilt Size: 62 1/2" x 87 1/2"

Block Size: 10" x 10"

Number of Blocks: 24

MATERIALS

- [ ] Light and dark prints to total 1 5/8 yards each for pieced blocks
- [ ] 2 1/8 yards black print for sashing strips and inner border
- [ ] 2 1/4 yards white-and-black print for outer border
- [ ] Batting 67" x 92"
- [ ] Backing 67" x 92"
- [ ] 9 yards self-made or purchased binding
- [ ] Coordinating all-purpose thread
- [ ] Basic sewing supplies and tools

unit as shown in Figure 1; press. Repeat for 48 Four-Patch units; press. Complete four Four-Patch units using black print and light print squares for borders.

Figure 1
Join 2 units to make
a Four-Patch unit.

STEP 4. Cut 24 squares each light and dark prints 5 1/2" x 5 1/2".

STEP 5. Join two same-fabric Four-Patch units with two same-fabric 5 1/2" x 5 1/2" squares to complete one block as shown in Figure 2; repeat for 24 blocks.

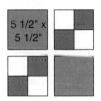

Figure 2
Join 2 Four-Patch units with 5 1/2"
squares to complete 1 block.

STEP 6. Cut 38 black print sashing strips 3" x 10 1/2".

STEP 7. Join four blocks with three sashing strips as shown in Figure 3 to make a row; press seams toward strips. *Note: Dark squares in Four-Patch units should*

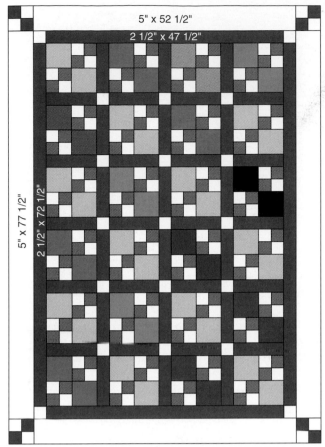

Double Four-Patch
Placement Diagram
62 1/2" x 87 1/2"

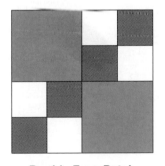

Double Four-Patch
10" x 10" Block

have the same alignment. Notice that one block on the sample quilt is

turned the wrong way. Repeat for six rows.

STEP 9. Join four sashing strips with three light print squares set aside in Step 2 to make a sashing row as shown in Figure 4; press seams toward squares. Repeat for five sashing rows. Join sashing rows alternately with block rows to complete pieced center. Press seams in one direction.

STEP 10. Sew 3" x 48" black print strips cut in Step 1 to shorter sides of pieced center. Press seams toward strips. Sew a light print square to each end of the 3" x 73" black print strips. Press seams toward squares. Sew a strip to opposite long sides of pieced center; press seams toward strips.

STEP 11. Cut two strips white-and-black print 5 1/2" x 53" along length of fabric; sew a strip to the shorter sides of the pieced center. Press seams toward strips. Cut two more strips white-and-black print 5 1/2" x 78" along length of fabric; sew a Four-Patch unit pieced in Step 3 for borders to each end of each strip. Press seams toward squares. Sew these strips to opposite long sides of pieced center; press seams toward strips.

STEP 12. Prepare quilt for quilting and finish referring to General Instructions, binding edges with self-made or purchased binding. ∎

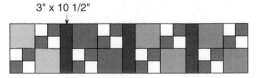

Figure 3
Join 4 blocks with 3 sashing strips to make a block row.

Figure 4
Join 4 sashing strips with three 3" squares to make a sashing row.

By Ruth Swasey

Snowball Quilt

Most quilters have enough scraps on hand to make many quilts. Scrap quilts work best if they are combined with a background fabric that is used throughout the quilt to tie everything together. In this quilt, muslin is that fabric—scraps make up the star designs.

INTERMEDIATE SKILL

SPECIFICATIONS
Quilt Size: 60" x 60"

Block Size: 6" x 6"

Number of Blocks: 64

MATERIALS
☐ 3/4 yard each pink and green prints for border

☐ 2 yards total medium to dark scraps

☐ 4 yards muslin

☐ Backing 64" x 64"

☐ Batting 64" x 64"

☐ 7 yards self-made or purchased binding

☐ Neutral color all-purpose thread

☐ Basic sewing supplies and tools

INSTRUCTIONS

STEP 1. Prepare templates for blocks and borders using pattern pieces given. Cut as directed on D and E for one block; repeat for 64 blocks. Cut as directed on pieces A, B and C for borders; set aside.

STEP 2. To piece one block, join four E pieces, sewing only to the end of the marked seam allowance. Set in D pieces as shown in Figure 1 to complete one block; repeat for 64 blocks. Press and square up to 6 1/2" x 6 1/2".

STEP 3. Arrange blocks in eight rows of eight blocks each. Join blocks in rows; join rows to complete pieced center. Press seams in one direction.

STEP 4. To piece border sections, sew a pink print C to a green print CR, sewing only to the end of the marked seam allowance; set in muslin B pieces as shown in Figure 2. Press; repeat for 32 units.

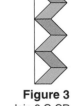

Figure 1
Set in D pieces.

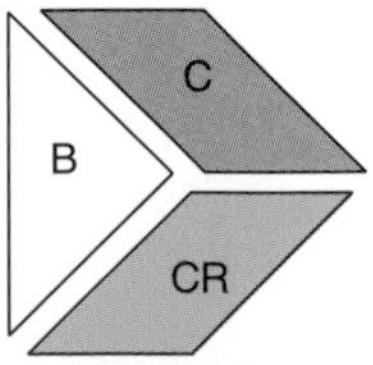

Figure 2
Set in B pieces to complete 1 border unit.

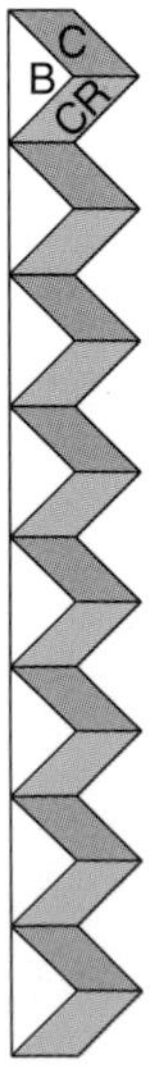

Figure 3
Join 8 C-CR-B units as shown.

STEP 5. Join eight C-CR-B units to make a strip as shown in Figure 3; repeat for four strips.

STEP 6. Sew a pieced strip to each side of the pieced center; press.

STEP 7. To make corner units, sew C to CR; set in two B pieces and A as shown in Figure 4. Sew one of these units to each corner of the pieced quilt to complete quilt top.

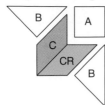

Figure 4
Sew C to CR; set in A and B
pieces to make corner units.

STEP 8. Prepare quilt top for quilting and finish referring to the General Instructions. ∎

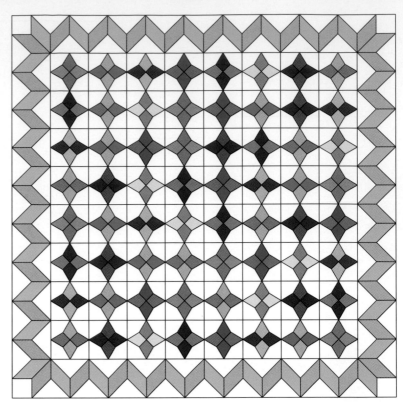

Snowball Quilt
Placement Diagram
60" x 60"

Snowball
6" x 6" Block

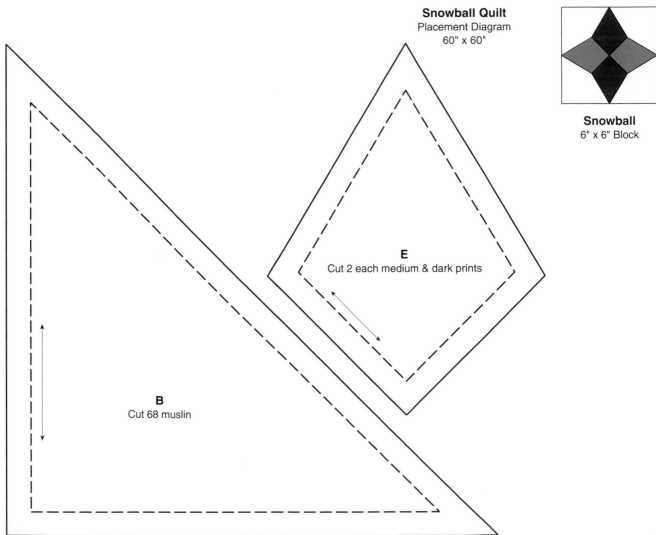

E
Cut 2 each medium & dark prints

B
Cut 68 muslin

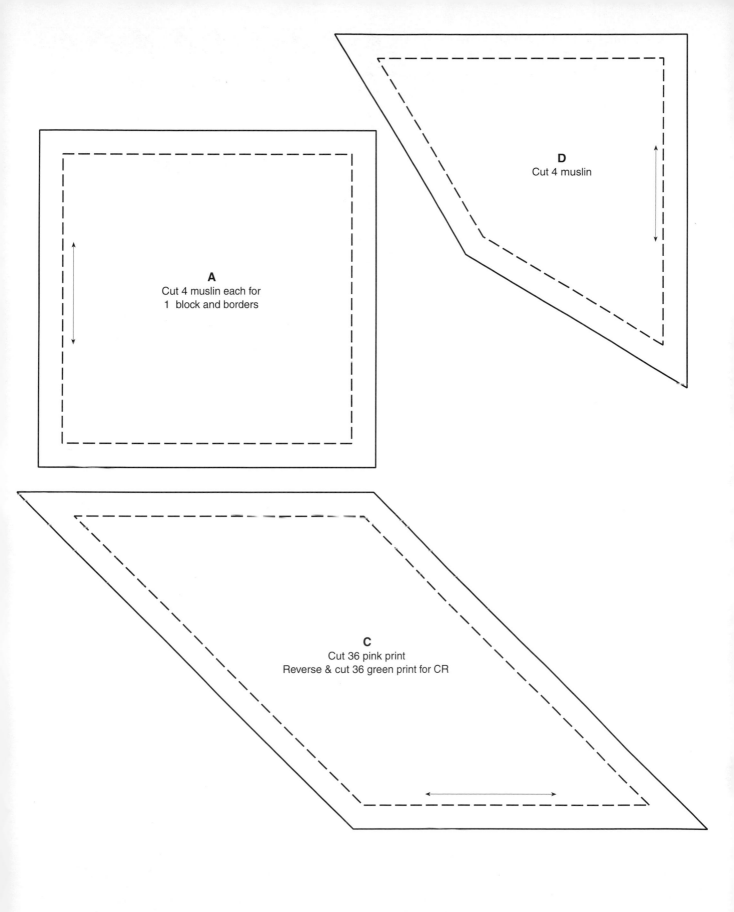

A
Cut 4 muslin each for
1 block and borders

D
Cut 4 muslin

C
Cut 36 pink print
Reverse & cut 36 green print for CR

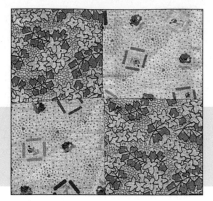

By Jill Reber

Midnight Stars

Use of lights and darks with different colors changes the pattern formed in any block. In this quilt the Four-Patch units are secondary to the lavender in the design.

INTERMEDIATE SKILL

SPECIFICATIONS
Quilt Size: 74 1/2" x 88"

Block Size: 12" x 12"

Number of Blocks: 20

MATERIALS
☐ 1 1/4 yards each lavender solid and print
☐ 2 yards each white and pink prints
☐ 2 1/4 yards pink floral
☐ Backing 79" x 92"
☐ Batting 79" x 92"
☐ 9 1/2 yards self-made or purchased binding
☐ Neutral color all-purpose thread
☐ Basic sewing supplies and tools, rotary cutter, ruler and cutting mat

INSTRUCTIONS
STEP 1. Cut five strips each pink floral and lavender solid 4 7/8" by fabric width. Subcut each strip into 4 7/8" square

segments; you will need 40 of each color. Cut each square in half on one diagonal to make 80 A triangles of each color.

STEP 2. Sew a pink floral A triangle to a lavender solid A triangle to make a triangle/square unit; repeat for 80 units.

STEP 3. Cut three strips pink floral 4 1/2" by fabric width. Subcut into 4 1/2"-square units to make 20 B squares.

STEP 4. Cut 10 strips each pink and white prints 2 1/2" by fabric width. Sew a pink print strip to a white print strip; press seam toward pink print. Repeat for 10 strip sets. Subcut strip sets into 2 1/2" units.

STEP 5. Join two pieced units to make a Four-Patch as shown in Figure 1; press. Repeat for 80 Four-Patch units.

STEP 6. Arrange four Four-Patch units with four A triangle/square units and one B square as shown in Figure 2. Join units in rows; join rows to complete one block. Press seams in one direction; repeat for 20 blocks.

Figure 1
Join 2 pieced units to
make a Four-Patch unit.

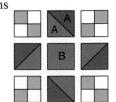

Figure 2
Arrange units in rows; join
rows to complete 1 block.

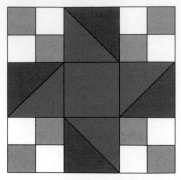

Midnight Stars
12" x 12" Block

STEP 7. Cut three strips pink floral 12 1/2" by fabric width. Subcut into 2" segments for sashing. You will need 49 sashing strips.

STEP 8. Cut two strips lavender print 2" by fabric width. Subcut into 2"-square segments for sashing squares. You will need 30 squares.

STEP 9. Join four blocks with five sashing strips to make a block row as shown in Figure 3; press seams toward strips. Repeat for five rows.

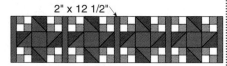
2" x 12 1/2"

Figure 3
Join 4 blocks with 5 sashing strips to make a block row.

STEP 10. Join five sashing squares with four sashing strips to make a sashing row as shown in Figure 4; press seams toward squares. Repeat for six sashing rows.

2" x 12 1/2"   2" x 2"

Figure 4
Join 5 squares with 4 sashing strips to make a sashing row.

STEP 11. Arrange sashing rows with block rows, beginning and ending with sashing rows. Join rows to complete pieced center. Press seams toward sashing rows.

STEP 12. Cut and piece two strips each 2" x 69 1/2" and 2" x 59" lavender solid. Sew the longer

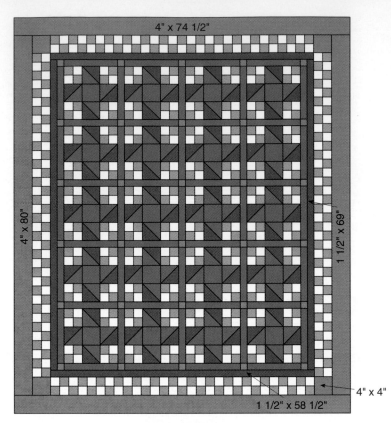

4" x 74 1/2"

4" x 80"

1 1/2" x 69"

4" x 4"

1 1/2" x 58 1/2"

Midnight Stars
Placement Diagram
74 1/2" x 88"

strips to opposite long sides and the shorter strips to the top and bottom of pieced center; press seams toward strips.

STEP 13. Cut 16 strips each pink and white prints 2 1/2" by fabric width. Join strips together along length; press seams toward pink print. Subcut into 2 1/2" segments. You will need 130 segments.

STEP 14. Sew two segments to make a Four-Patch unit again referring to Figure 1; repeat for 64 units.

STEP 15. Join 14 Four-Patch units to make a strip; repeat. Add one pieced segment to one end of each strip as shown in Figure 5;

Figure 5
Sew a pieced segment to one end of the Four-Patch row.

press seams in one direction. Sew a pieced strip to top and bottom of pieced center. *Note: Pieced strip is 1/2" shorter than lavender solid border. Carefully stretch the pieced strip to same length while sewing.* Press seams toward strip.

STEP 16. Join 18 Four-Patch units to make a strip; repeat. Cut four squares lavender print 4 1/2" x 4 1/2"; sew a square to each end of each pieced strip. Sew strips to opposite long sides of pieced center; press seams toward strips.

STEP 17. Cut and piece two strips each 4 1/2" x 80 1/2" and 4 1/2" x 75" lavender print. Sew the longer strips to opposite long sides and the shorter strips to the top and bottom of pieced center; press seams toward strips.

STEP 18. Prepare quilt top for quilting and finish referring to the General Instructions. ■

By Sandra L. Hatch

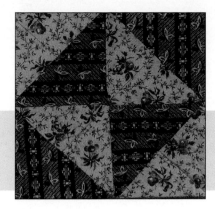

Broken Dishes

The Broken Dishes blocks in this quilt were among scraps
and blocks found in a box purchased at a yard sale. The
blocks were hand-pieced. Putting them together was a challenge. Making a copy of the quilt would be fun and easy.

PROJECT NOTES

The problem with acquiring a bunch of old blocks
is what to do with them. Historians would have
you keep them as blocks forever, just as they are. I
prefer to work with them and make something use-
ful. The process of trying to plan a project is challenging.

There were 34 blocks in this bunch—I needed 36
to make the quilt as shown. I made two new blocks
using reproduction fabrics. Can you pick them out?
They are not the corner blocks, although those look
bright and new.

I had to decide whether to use the pink blocks.
Almost all of the other blocks are brown or beige.
The pink stands out like a sore thumb. I decided
that was what the original maker made, and I
would use them.

Choosing fabrics to set the blocks together was
another challenge. I selected the brown because it
went well with the pieced blocks.
Now that it is finished, I think it works with the
fabrics I chose, and I like the finished quilt.

INSTRUCTIONS

STEP 1. Cut 72 squares 4 3/8" x 4 3/8" each
light and dark prints. *Note: If using scraps, you need
two squares of the same light and dark fabrics for each
block.* Cut each square in half on one diagonal to
make triangles. Sew a light triangle to a dark

INTERMEDIATE SKILL

SPECIFICATIONS
Quilt Size: 70" x 70"

Block Size: 7" x 7"

Number of Blocks: 36

MATERIALS
- ☐ 1 yard total each light
  and dark prints for
  pieced blocks

- ☐ 2 yards brown print for
  setting blocks and outer
  border

- ☐ 1 yard navy print for
  inner border

- ☐ Batting 74" x 74"

- ☐ Backing 74" x 74"

- ☐ 8 yards self-made or
  purchased binding

- ☐ Coordinating all-pur-
  pose thread

- ☐ Basic sewing supplies
  and tools

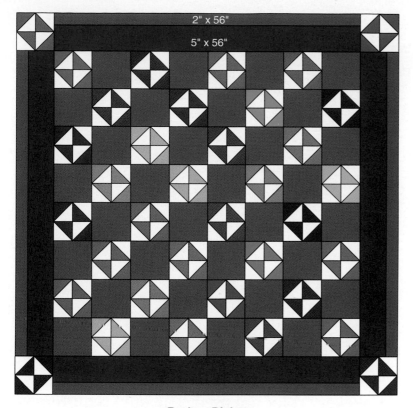

Broken Dishes
Placement Diagram
70" x 70"

Broken Dishes
7" x 7" Block

blocks with four squares to make a row as shown in Figure 2; repeat for eight rows, referring to the Placement Diagram.

STEP 4. Arrange blocks in eight rows of eight blocks each, beginning every other row with a pieced block. Join blocks in rows; join rows to complete pieced top. Press seams in one direction.

STEP 5. Cut four strips each navy print 5 1/2" x 56 1/2" and brown print 2 1/2" x 56 1/2". Sew a navy strip to a brown strip; press seams toward navy print. Repeat for four strips.

STEP 6. Sew a pieced strip to opposite sides of the pieced top; press seams toward strips. Sew a pieced block to each end of the remaining two strips, referring to Placement Diagram. Sew these strips to the remaining sides of the pieced top; press seams toward strips.

STEP 7. Prepare quilt for quilting and finish referring to General Instructions, binding edges with self-made or purchased binding. ■

triangle to make one triangle/square unit. Repeat for 144 units.

Figure 1
Join 4 same-fabric
triangle/squares to
make a block.

STEP 2. Join four same-fabric triangle/square units to make one block as shown in Figure 1; press. Repeat for 36 squares.

STEP 3. Cut 32 squares brown print 7 1/2" x 7 1/2". Join four

Figure 2
Join 4 blocks with 4 squares to make a row.

By Janice McKee

Stars & Stripes

When you think of stars and stripes you probably visualize red, white and blue. In this quilt, the colors are not what you expect—scraps of every color are used. The only requirement is that there be true value changes from light to medium to dark.

INTERMEDIATE SKILL

SPECIFICATIONS
Quilt Size: 59" x 59"

Block Size: 12" x 12"

Number of Blocks: 16

MATERIALS
- ☐ 2/3 yard dark scraps
- ☐ 1 1/4 yards medium scraps
- ☐ 1 3/4 yards navy print for borders
- ☐ 2 yards light scraps
- ☐ Backing 63" x 63"
- ☐ Batting 63" x 63"
- ☐ 7 yards self-made or purchased binding
- ☐ Neutral color all-purpose thread
- ☐ Basic sewing supplies and tools and water-erasable marker

INSTRUCTIONS

STEP 1. Prepare templates using pattern pieces given. Cut as directed on each piece for one block; repeat for 12 blocks.

STEP 2. To piece one block, sew B and BR to A; add C, D and DR referring to Figure 1; repeat for four units. Join four units to complete one block as shown in Figure 2; repeat for 16 blocks. Press and square up blocks to 12 1/2" x 12 1/2", if necessary.

Figure 1
Sew B and BR to A;
add C, D and DR to
complete 1 unit.

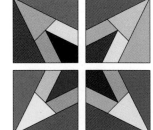

Figure 2
Join 4 units to complete 1 block.

STEP 3. Arrange blocks in four rows of four blocks each. Join blocks in rows; join rows to complete pieced center. Press seams in one direction.

STEP 4. Cut four strips navy print 6" x 59 1/2" from fabric length. Sew a strip to each side of the pieced center, mitering corners; press seams toward strips.

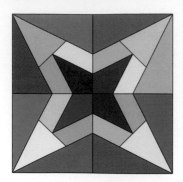

Stars & Stripes
12" x 12" Block

STEP 5. Mark Star Quilting Design given in border strips using water-erasable marker. Refer to Figure 3 for suggested quilting design for blocks.

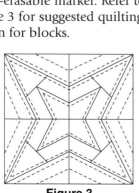

Figure 3
Suggested quilting design for blocks.

STEP 6. Prepare quilt top for quilting and finish referring to the General Instructions. ■

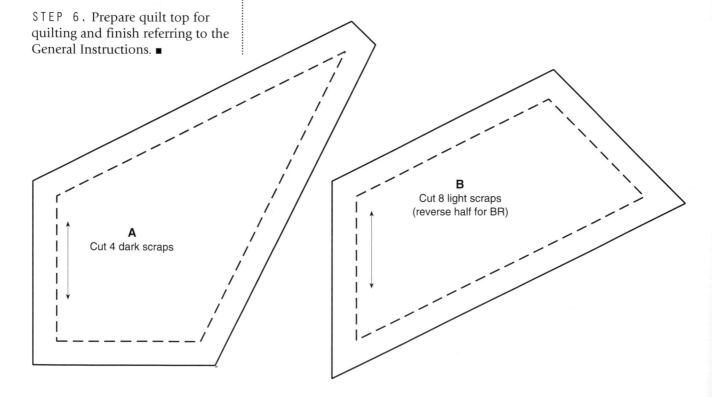

5 1/2" x 59"

Stars & Stripes
Placement Diagram
59" x 59"

A
Cut 4 dark scraps

B
Cut 8 light scraps
(reverse half for BR)

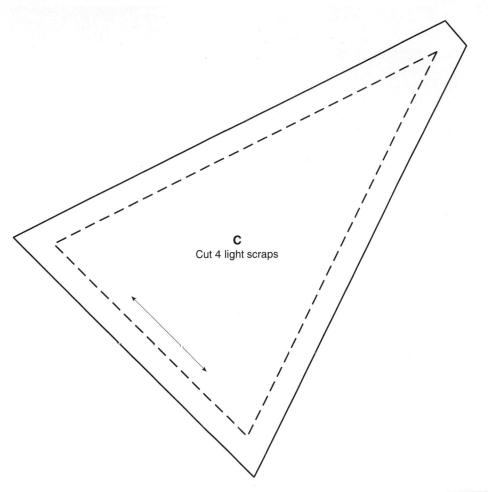

C
Cut 4 light scraps

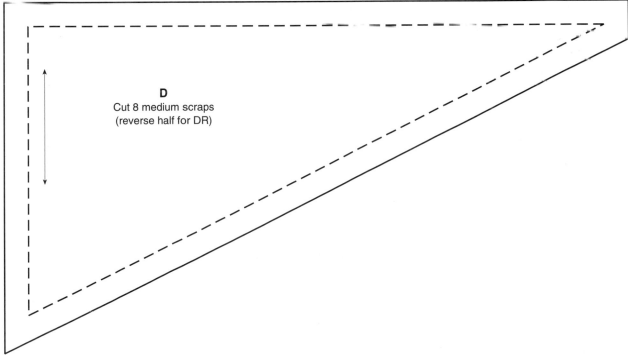

D
Cut 8 medium scraps
(reverse half for DR)

By Jill Reber

Chutes & Ladders

Chutes & Ladders was inspired by an antique quilt I saw at a flea market. I chose to use reproduction prints to give my version an antique scrappy look.

INTERMEDIATE SKILL

SPECIFICATIONS

Quilt Size: 78" x 94"

Block Size: 16" x 16"

Number of Blocks: 20

MATERIALS

☐ 1/4 yard each 10 different medium pink prints

☐ 1/4 yard each 10 different brown prints

☐ 11 1/2 yards brown print for borders

☐ 3 1/2 yards cream print for background

☐ Backing 82" x 98"

☐ Batting 82" x 98"

☐ Neutral color all-purpose thread

☐ Basic sewing supplies and tools, rotary cutter, ruler and cutting mat

INSTRUCTIONS

STEP 1. To make Four-Patch units, cut 20 strips 2 1/2" by fabric width cream print. Subcut into forty 2 1/2" x 22" strips. Cut two strips each 2 1/2" by fabric width from the 10 different pink prints for a total of 20 strips. Subcut into forty 2 1/2" x 22" strips.

STEP 2. Sew one pink print strip to one cream print strip; press seams toward pink strip. Repeat with all 40 strips. Subcut strips into 2 1/2" units. You will need 320 units.

STEP 3. Join two units pieced in Step 2 to make a Four-Patch unit, choosing random units; repeat for 160 units.

STEP 4. To make B triangle/square units, cut 10 strips cream print 4 7/8" by fabric width. Subcut into 80 squares 4 7/8" x 4 7/8". Cut one strip each 4 7/8" by fabric width from the 10 different brown prints for a total of 10 strips. Subcut into 80 squares 4 7/8" x 4 7/8".

STEP 5. Cut each 4 7/8" x 4 7/8" square on one diagonal to make B triangles. Sew a cream print triangle to a brown print triangle to make a B triangle/square; repeat for 160 B units.

STEP 6. Join two Four-Patch units with two B units as shown in Figure 1 to make C units; repeat for 80 C units.

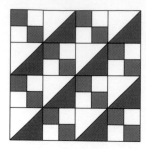

Chutes & Ladders
16" x 16" Block

STEP 7. Join four C units to complete one block as shown in Figure 2; repeat for 20 blocks. Press and square up blocks to 16 1/2" x 16 1/2" if necessary.

Figure 1
Join 2 Four-Patch units with 2 B units to make C units.

Figure 2
Join 4 C units to complete 1 block.

STEP 8. Arrange blocks in five rows of four blocks each; join blocks in rows. Join rows; press seams in one direction to complete pieced center.

STEP 9. Cut and piece two strips cream print 2 1/2" x 64 1/2" and

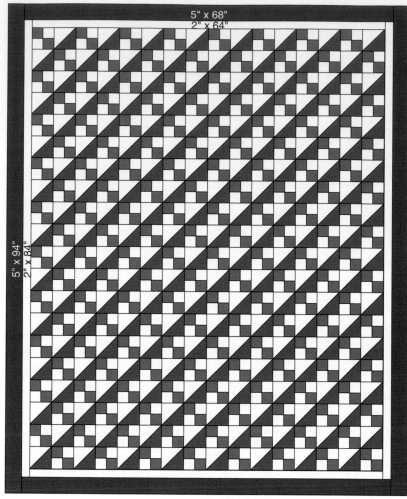

Chutes & Ladders
Placement Diagram
78" x 94"

two strips 2 1/2" x 84 1/2". Sew the shorter strips to the top and bottom and longer strips to opposite sides of the pieced center; press seams toward strips.

STEP 10. Cut two strips brown print 5 1/2" x 68 1/2" and two strips 5 1/2" x 94 1/2". Sew the shorter strips to the top and bottom and longer strips to opposite

sides of the pieced center; press seams toward strips.

STEP 11. Cut 2"-wide random length strips from leftover pink prints. Join on short ends to make a 10-yard long strip for binding.

STEP 12. Prepare quilt top for quilting and finish referring to the General Instructions. ■

Quiltmaking Basics

Materials & Supplies

FABRICS

Fabric Choices. Four-Patch quilts combine fabrics of many types, depending on the quilt. It is best to combine same-fiber-content fabrics when making Four-Patch quilts.

Buying Fabrics. One hundred percent cotton fabrics are recommended for making quilts. Choose colors similar to those used in the quilts shown or colors of your own preference. Most Four-Patch quilt designs depend more on contrast of values than on the colors used to create the design.

Preparing the Fabric for Use. Fabrics may be prewashed or not depending on your preference. Whether you do or don't, be sure your fabrics are colorfast and won't run onto each other when washed after use.

Fabric Grain. Fabrics are woven with threads going in a crosswise and lengthwise direction. The threads cross at right angles—the more threads per inch, the stronger the fabric.

The crosswise threads will stretch a little. The lengthwise threads will not stretch at all. Cutting the fabric at a 45-degree angle to the crosswise and lengthwise threads produces a bias edge which stretches a great deal when pulled (Figure 1).

If templates are given with patterns in this book, pay careful attention to the grain lines marked with arrows. These arrows indicate that the piece should be placed on the lengthwise grain with the arrow running on one thread. Although it is not necessary to examine the fabric and find a thread to match to, it is important to try to place the arrow with the lengthwise grain of the fabric (Figure 2).

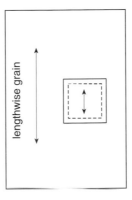

Figure 2
Place the template with marked arrow on the lengthwise grain of the fabric.

THREAD

For most piecing, good-quality cotton or cotton-covered polyester is the thread of choice. Inexpensive polyester threads are not recommended because they can cut the fibers of cotton fabrics.

Choose a color thread that will match or blend with the fabrics in your quilt. For quilts pieced with dark and light color fabrics choose a neutral thread color, such as a medium gray, as a compromise between colors. Test by pulling a sample seam.

BATTING

Batting is the material used to give a quilt loft or thickness. It also adds warmth.

Batting size is listed in inches for each pattern to reflect the size needed to complete the quilt according to the instructions.

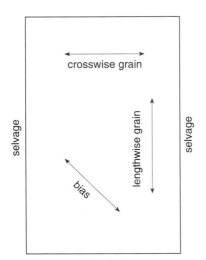

Figure 1
Drawing shows lengthwise, crosswise and bias threads.

Purchase the size large enough to cut the size you need for the quilt of your choice.

Some qualities to look for in batting are drapeability, resistance to fiber migration, loft and softness.

If you are unsure which kind of batting to use, purchase the smallest size batting available in the type you'd like to try. Test each sample on a small project. Choose the batting that you like working with most and that will result in the type of quilt you need.

TOOLS & EQUIPMENT

There are few truly essential tools and little equipment required for quiltmaking. The basics include needles (hand-sewing and quilting betweens), pins (long, thin sharp pins are best), sharp scissors or shears, a thimble, template materials (plastic or cardboard), marking tools (chalk marker, water-erasable pen and a No. 2 pencil are a few) and a quilting frame or hoop. For piecing and/or quilting by machine, add a sewing machine to the list.

Other sewing basics such as a seam ripper, pincushion, measuring tape and an iron are also necessary. For choosing colors or quilting designs for your quilt, or for designing your own quilt, it is helpful to have on hand graph paper, tracing paper, colored pencils or markers and a ruler.

For making Four-Patch quilts, a rotary cutter, mat and specialty rulers are often used. We recommend an ergonomic rotary cutter, a large self-healing mat and several rulers. If you can choose only one size, a 6" x 24" marked in 1/8" or 1/4" increments is recommended.

Construction Methods

TEMPLATES

Traditional Templates. While some quilt instructions in this book use rotary-cut strips and quick sewing methods, a few patterns require templates. Templates are like the pattern pieces used to sew a garment. They are used to cut the fabric

pieces which make up the quilt top. There are two types—templates that include a 1/4" seam allowance and those that don't.

Choose the template material and the pattern. Transfer the pattern shapes to the template material with a sharp No. 2 lead pencil. Write the pattern name, piece letter or number, grain line and number to cut for one block or whole quilt on each piece as shown in Figure 3.

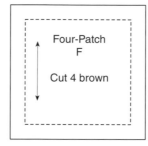

Figure 3
Mark each template with the pattern name and piece identification.

Some patterns require a reversed piece (Figure 4). These patterns are labeled with an R after the piece letter; for example, F and FR. To reverse a template, first cut it with the labeled side up and then with the labeled side down. Compare these to the right and left fronts of a blouse. When making a garment, you accomplish reversed pieces when cutting the pattern on two layers of fabric placed with right sides together. This can be done when cutting templates as well.

If cutting one layer of fabric at a time, first trace the template onto the backside of the fabric with the marked side down; turn the template over with the marked side up to make reverse pieces.

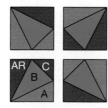

Figure 4
This pattern uses reversed pieces.

Appliqué patterns given in this book do not include a seam allowance.

Most designs are given in one drawing rather than individual pieces. This saves space while giving you the complete design to trace on the background block to help with placement of the pieces later. Make templates for each shape using the drawing for exact size. Remember to label each piece as for piecing templates.

For hand appliqué, add a seam allowance when cutting pieces from fabric. You may trace the template with label side up on the right side of the fabric if you are careful to mark lightly. The traced line is then the guide for turning the edges under when stitching.

If you prefer to mark on the wrong side of the fabric, turn the template over if you want the pattern to face the same way it does on the page.

For machine appliqué, a seam allowance is not necessary. Trace template onto the right side of the fabric with label facing up. Cut around shape on the traced line.

PIECING

Hand-Piecing Basics. When hand-piecing it is easier to begin with templates which do not include the 1/4" seam allowance. Place the template on the wrong side of the fabric, lining up the marked grain line with lengthwise or crosswise fabric grain. If the piece does not have to be reversed, place with labeled side up. Trace around shape; move, leaving 1/2" between the shapes, and mark again.

When you have marked the appropriate number of pieces, cut out pieces, leaving 1/4" beyond marked line all around each piece.

To piece, refer to assembly drawings to piece units and blocks, if provided. To join two units, place the patches with right sides together. Stick a pin

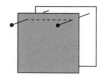

Figure 5
Stick a pin through fabrics to match the beginning of the seam.

in at the beginning of the seam through both fabric patches, matching the beginning points (Figure 5); for hand-piecing, the seam begins on the traced line, not at the edge of the fabric (see Figure 6).

Figure 6
Begin hand-piecing at seam, not at the edge of the fabric. Continue stitching along seam line.

Thread a sharp needle; knot one strand of the thread at the end. Remove the pin and insert the needle in the hole; make a short stitch and then a backstitch right over the first stitch. Continue making short stitches with several stitches on the needle at one time. As you stitch, check the back piece often to assure accurate stitching on the seam line. Take a stitch at the end of the seam; backstitch and knot at the same time as shown in Figure 7.

Seams on hand-pieced fabric patches may be finger-pressed toward the darker fabric.

To sew units together, pin fabric patches together, matching seams. Sew as above except where seams meet; at these intersections, backstitch, go through seam to next piece and backstitch again to secure seam joint.

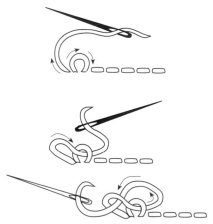

Figure 7
Make a loop in a backstitch to make a knot.

Not all pieced blocks can be stitched with straight seams or in rows.

Some patterns require set-in pieces. To begin a set-in seam on a star pattern, pin one side of the square to the proper side of the star point with right sides together, matching corners. Start stitching at the seam line on the outside point; stitch on the marked seam line to the end of the seam line at the center referring to Figure 8.

Bring around the adjacent side and pin to the next star point, matching seams. Continue the stitching line from the adjacent seam through corners and to the outside edge of the square as shown in Figure 9.

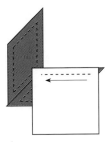

Figure 8
To set a square into a diamond point, match seams and stitch from outside edge to center.

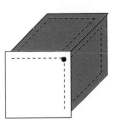

Figure 9
Continue stitching the adjacent side of the square to the next diamond shape in 1 seam from center to outside as shown.

Machine-Piecing. If making templates, include the 1/4" seam allowance on the template for machine-piecing. Place template on the wrong side of the fabric as for hand-piecing except butt pieces against one another when tracing.

Set machine on 2.5 or 12–15 stitches per inch. Join pieces as for hand-piecing for set-in seams; but for other straight seams, begin and end sewing at the end of the fabric patch sewn as shown in Figure 10. No

backstitching is necessary when machine-stitching.

Join units as for hand-piecing referring to the piecing diagrams where needed. Chain piecing (Figure 11—sewing several like units before sewing other units) saves time by eliminating beginning and ending stitches.

When joining machine-pieced units, match seams against each other with seam allowances pressed in opposite directions to reduce bulk and make perfect matching of seams possible (Figure 12).

Figure 10
Begin machine-piecing at the end of the piece, not at the end of the seam.

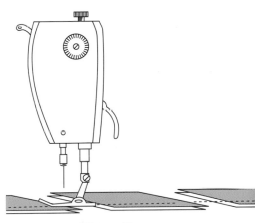

Figure 11
Units may be chain-pieced to save time.

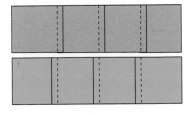

Figure 12
Sew machine-pieced units with seams pressed in opposite directions.

CUTTING

Quick-Cutting. Quick-cutting and piecing strips is recommended for making many of the Four-Patch quilts in this book. Templates are completely eliminated; instead, a rotary cutter, plastic ruler and mat are used to cut fabric pieces.

When rotary-cutting strips, straighten raw edges of fabric by folding fabric in fourths across the width as shown in Figure 13. Press down flat; place ruler on fabric square with edge of fabric and make one cut from the folded edge to the outside edge. If strips are not straightened, a wavy strip will result as shown in Figure 14. Always cut away from your body, holding the ruler firmly with the non-cutting hand. Keep fingers away from the edge of the ruler as it is easy for the rotary cutter to slip and jump over the edge of the ruler if cutting is not properly done.

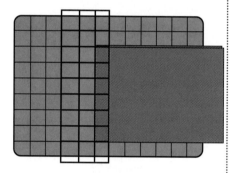

Figure 13
Fold fabric and straighten as shown.

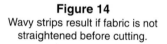

Figure 14
Wavy strips result if fabric is not straightened before cutting.

For many Four-Patch blocks two strips are stitched together as shown in Figure 15. The strips are stitched, pressed and cut into segments as shown in Figure 16.

The cut segments are arranged as shown in Figure 17 and stitched to complete one Four-Patch block. Although the block shown is very simple, the same methods may be used for more complicated patterns.

The direction to press seams on strip sets is important for accurate piecing later. The normal rule for pressing is to press seams toward the darker fabric to keep the colors from showing through on lighter colors later. For joining segments from strip sets,

this rule doesn't always apply.

It is best if seams on adjacent rows are pressed in opposite directions. When aligning segments to stitch rows together, if pressed properly, seam joints will have a seam going in both directions as shown in Figure 18.

If a square is required for the pattern, it can be sub-cut from a strip as shown in Figure 19.

Figure 15
Join 2 strips as shown.

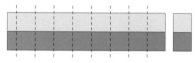

Figure 16
Cut segments from the stitched strip set.

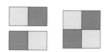

Figure 17
Arrange cut segments to make a Four-Patch block.

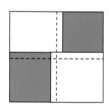

Figure 18
Seams go in both directions at seam joints.

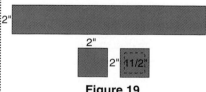

Figure 19
If cutting squares, cut proper-width strip into same-width segments. Here, a 2" strip is cut into 2" segments to create 2" squares. These squares finish at 1 1/2" when sewn.

If you need right triangles with the straight grain on the short sides, you can use the same method, but you need to figure out how wide to cut the strip. Measure the finished size of one short side of the triangle. Add 7/8" to this size for seam allowance. Cut fabric strips this width; cut the strips into the same increment to create squares. Cut the squares on the diagonal to produce triangles. For example, if you need a triangle with a 2" finished height, cut the strips 2 7/8" by the width of the fabric. Cut the strips into 2 7/8" squares. Cut each square on the diagonal to produce the correct-size triangle with the grain on the short sides (Figure 20).

Figure 20
Cut 2" (finished size) triangles from 2 7/8" squares as shown.

Triangles sewn together to make squares are called half-square triangles or triangle/squares. When joined, the triangle/square unit has the straight of grain on all outside edges of the block.

Another method of making triangle/squares is shown in Figure 21. Layer two squares with right sides together; draw a diagonal line through the center. Stitch 1/4" on both sides of the line. Cut apart on the drawn line to reveal two stitched triangle/squares.

Figure 21
Mark a diagonal line on the square; stitch 1/4" on each side of the line. Cut on line to reveal stitched triangle/squares.

If you need triangles with the straight of grain on the diagonal, such as for fill-in triangles on the outside edges of a diagonal-set quilt, the procedure is a bit different.

To make these triangles, a square is cut on both diagonals; thus, the straight of grain is on the longest or diagonal side (Figure 22). To figure out the size to cut the square, add 1 1/4" to the needed finished size of the longest side of the triangle. For example, if you need a triangle with a 12" finished diagonal, cut a 13 1/4" square.

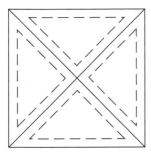

Figure 22
Add 1 1/4" to the finished size of the longest side of the triangle needed and cut on both diagonals to make a quarter-square triangle.

If templates are given, use their measurements to cut fabric strips to correspond with that measurement. The template may be used on the strip to cut pieces quickly. Strip cutting works best for squares, triangles, rectangles and diamonds. Odd shaped templates are difficult to cut in multiple layers using a rotary cutter.

FOUNDATION PIECING

Foundation Piecing. Paper or fabric foundation pieces are used to make very accurate blocks, provide stability for weak fabrics, and add body and weight to the finished quilt.

Temporary foundation materials include paper, tracing paper, freezer paper and removable interfacing. Permanent foundations include

TIPS & TECHNIQUES

If you cannot see the lines on the backside of the paper when paper-piecing, draw over lines with a small felt-tip marker. The lines should now be visible on the backside to help with placement of fabric pieces.

utility fabrics, non-woven interfacing, flannel, fleece and batting.

Methods of marking foundations include basting lines, pencils or pens, needlepunching, tracing wheel, hot-iron transfers, copy machine, premarked, stamps or stencils.

There are two methods of foundation piecing—under-piecing and top-piecing. When under-piecing, the pattern is reversed when tracing. We have not included any patterns for top-piecing. *Note: All patterns for which we recommend paper piecing are already reversed in full-size drawings given.*

To under-piece, place a scrap of fabric larger than the lined space on the unlined side of the paper in the No. 1 position. Place piece 2 right sides together with piece 1; pin on seam line, and fold back to check that the piece will cover space 2 before stitching.

Stitch along line on the lined side of the paper—fabric will not be visible. Sew several stitches beyond the beginning and ending of the line. Backstitching is not required as another fabric seam will cover this seam.

Remove pin; finger-press piece 2 flat. Continue adding all pieces in numerical order in the same manner until all pieces are stitched to paper. Trim excess to outside line (1/4" larger all around than finished size of the block).

Tracing paper can be used as a temporary foundation. It is removed when blocks are complete and stitched together. To paper-piece, copy patterns given here using a copy machine or trace each block individually. Measure the finished paper foundations to insure accuracy in copying.

APPLIQUÉ

Appliqué. Appliqué is the process of applying one piece of fabric on top of another for decorative or functional purposes.

Making Templates. Most appliqué designs given here are given as full-size drawings for the completed

designs. The drawings show dotted lines to indicate where one piece overlaps another. Other marks indicate placement of embroidery stitches for decorative purposes such as eyes, lips, flowers, etc.

For hand appliqué, trace each template onto the right side of the fabric with template right side up. Cut around shape, adding a 1/8"–1/4" seam allowance.

Before the actual appliqué process begins, cut the background block and prepare it for stitching. Most appliqué designs are centered on the block. To find the center of the background square, fold it in half and in half again; crease with your fingers. Now unfold and fold diagonally and crease; repeat for other corners referring to Figure 23.

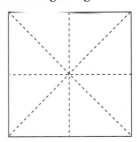

Figure 23
Fold background to mark centers as shown.

Center-line creases help position the design. If centering the appliqué design is important, an X has been placed on each drawing to mark the center of the design. Match the X with the creased center of the background block when placing pieces. If you have a full-size drawing of the design, as is given with most appliqué designs in this book, it might help you to draw on the background block to help with placement.

Transfer the design to a large piece of tracing paper. Place the paper on top of the design; use masking tape to hold in place. Trace design onto paper.

If you don't have a light box, tape the pattern on a window; center the background block on top and tape in place. Trace the design onto the background block with a water-erasable marker or chalk pencil. This drawing will mark exactly where the fabric pieces should be placed on the background block.

Hand Appliqué. Traditional hand appliqué uses a template made from the desired finished shape without seam allowance added.

After fabric is prepared, trace the desired shape onto the right side of the fabric with a water-erasable marker, light lead or chalk pencil. Leave at least 1/2" between design motifs when tracing to allow for the seam allowance when cutting out the shapes.

When the desired number of shapes needed has been drawn on the fabric pieces, cut out shapes leaving 1/8"–1/4" all around drawn line for turning under.

Turn the shape's edges over on the drawn or stitched line. When turning the edges under, make sharp corners sharp and smooth edges smooth. The fabric patch should retain the shape of the template used to cut it.

When turning in concave curves, clip to seams and baste the seam allowance over as shown in Figure 24.

Figure 24
Concave curves should be clipped before turning as shown.

During the actual appliqué process, you may be layering one shape on top of another. Where two fabrics overlap, the underneath piece does not have to be turned under or stitched down.

If possible, trim away the underneath fabric when the block is finished by carefully cutting away the background from underneath and then cutting away unnecessary layers to reduce bulk and avoid shadows from darker fabrics showing through on light fabrics.

For hand appliqué, position the fabric shapes on the background block and pin or baste them in place. Using a blind stitch or appliqué stitch, sew pieces in place with matching thread and small stitches. Start with background pieces first and work up to foreground pieces. Appliqué the pieces in place on the background in numerical order, if given, layering as necessary.

Machine Appliqué. There are several products available to help make the machine-appliqué process easier and faster.

Fusible transfer web is a commercial product similar to iron-on interfacings except it has two sticky sides. It is used to adhere appliqué shapes to the background with heat. Paper is adhered to one side of the web.

To use, dry-iron the sticky side of the fusible product onto the wrong side of the chosen fabric. Draw desired shapes onto the paper and cut them out. Peel off the paper and dry-iron the shapes in place on the background fabric. The shape will stay in place while you stitch around it. This process adds a little bulk or stiffness to the appliquéd shape and makes quilting through the layers by hand difficult.

For successful machine appliqué a tear-off stabilizer is recommended. This product is placed under the background fabric while machine appliqué is being done. It is torn away when the work is finished. This kind of stabilizer keeps the background fabric from pulling during the machine-appliqué process.

During the actual machine-appliqué process, you will be layering one shape on top of another. Where two fabrics overlap, the underneath piece does not have to be turned under or stitched down.

Thread the top of the machine with thread to match the fabric patches or with threads that coordinate or contrast with fabrics. Rayon thread is a good choice when a sheen is desired on the finished appliqué stitches. Do not use rayon thread in the bobbin; use all-purpose thread.

Set your machine to make a zigzag stitch and practice on scraps of similar weight to check the tension. If you can see the bobbin thread on the top of the appliqué, adjust your machine to make a balanced stitch. Different-width stitches are available; choose one that will not overpower the appliqué shapes. In some cases these appliqué stitches will be used as decorative stitches as well and you may want the thread to show.

If using a stabilizer, place this under the background fabric and pin or fuse in place. Place shapes as for hand-appliqué and stitch all around shapes by machine.

When all machine work is complete, remove stabilizer from the back referring to the manufacturer's instructions.

TIPS & TECHNIQUES

Before machine-piecing fabric patches together, test your sewing machine for positioning an accurate 1/4" seam allowance. There are several tools to help guarantee this. Some machine needles may be moved to allow the presser-foot edge to be a 1/4" guide.

A special foot may be purchased for your machine that will guarantee an accurate 1/4" seam. A piece of masking tape can be placed on the throat plate of your sewing machine to mark the 1/4" seam. A plastic stick-on ruler may be used instead of tape with the same results.

Putting It All Together

Many steps are required to prepare a quilt top for quilting, including setting the blocks together, adding borders, choosing and marking quilting designs, layering the top, batting and backing for quilting, quilting or tying the layers and finishing the edges of the quilt.

As you begin the process of finishing your quilt top, strive for a neat, flat quilt with square sides and corners, not for perfection—that will come with time and practice.

Finishing the Top

Settings. Most quilts are made by sewing individual blocks together in rows which, when joined, create a design. There are several other methods used to join blocks. Sometimes the setting choice is determined by the block's design. For example, a house block should be placed upright on a quilt, not sideways or upside down.

Plain blocks can be alternated with pieced or appliquéd blocks in a straight set. Making a quilt using plain blocks saves time; half the number of pieced or appliquéd blocks are needed to make the same-size quilt as shown in Figure 1.

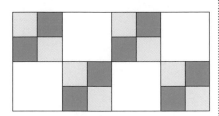

Figure 1
Alternate plain blocks with pieced blocks to save time.

Adding Borders. Borders are an integral part of the quilt and should complement the colors and designs used in the quilt center. Borders frame a quilt just like a mat and frame do a picture.

If fabric strips are added for borders, they may be mitered or butted at the corners as shown in Figures 2 and 3.

To determine the size for butted border strips, measure across the center of the completed quilt top from one side raw edge to the other side raw edge. This measurement will include a 1/4" seam allowance.

Cut two border strips that length by the chosen width of the border. Sew these strips to the top and bottom of the pieced center referring to Figure 4. Press the seam allowance toward the border strips.

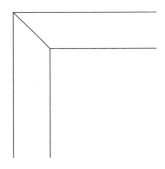

Figure 2
Mitered corners look like this.

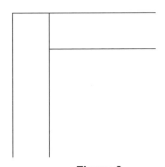

Figure 3
Butted corners look like this.

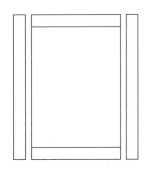

Figure 4
Sew border strips to opposite sides; sew remaining 2 strips to remaining sides to make butted corners.

Measure across the completed quilt top at the center, from top raw edge to bottom raw edge, including the two border strips already added. Cut two border strips that length by the

chosen width of the border. Sew a strip to each of the two remaining sides as shown in Figure 4. Press the seams toward the border strips.

To make mitered corners, measure the quilt as before. To this add twice the width of the border and 1/2" for seam allowances to determine the length of the strips. Repeat for opposite sides. Center and sew on each strip, stopping stitching 1/4" from corner, leaving the remainder of the strip dangling.

Press corners at a 45-degree angle to form a crease. Stitch from the inside quilt corner to the outside on the creased line. Trim excess away after stitching and press mitered seams open (Figures 5–7).

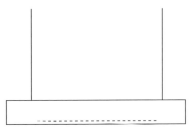

Figure 5
For mitered corner, stitch strip, stopping 1/4" from corner seam.

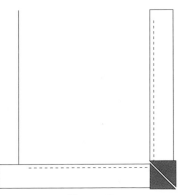

Figure 6
Fold and press corner to make a 45-degree angle.

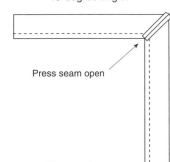

Press seam open

Figure 7
Trim away excess from underneath when stitching is complete. Press seams open.

Carefully press the entire piece, including the pieced center. Avoid pulling and stretching while pressing, which would distort shapes.

Getting Ready to Quilt

Choosing a Quilting Design. If you choose to hand- or machine-quilt your finished top, you will need to choose a design for quilting.

There are several types of quilting designs, some of which may not have to be marked. The easiest of the unmarked designs is in-the-ditch quilting. Here the quilting stitches are placed in the valley created by the seams joining two pieces together or next to the edge of an appliqué design. There is no need to mark a top for in-the-ditch quilting. Machine quilters choose this option because the stitches are not as obvious on the finished quilt (Figure 8).

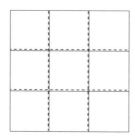

Figure 8
In-the-ditch quilting is done in the seam that joins 2 pieces.

Outline-quilting 1/4" or more away from seams or appliqué shapes is another no-mark alternative (Figure 9) which prevents having to sew through the layers made by seams, thus making stitching easier.

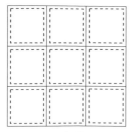

Figure 9
Outline-quilting 1/4" away from seam is a popular choice for quilting.

If you are not comfortable eyeballing the 1/4" (or other distance), masking tape is available in different widths and is helpful to place on straight-edge designs to mark the quilting line. If using masking tape, place the tape right up against the seam and quilt close to the other edge.

Meander or free-motion quilting by machine fills in open spaces and doesn't require marking. It is fun and easy to stitch as shown in Figure 10.

Figure 10
Machine meander quilting fills in large spaces.

Marking the Top for Quilting or Tying. If you choose a fancy or allover design for quilting, you will need to transfer the design to your quilt top before layering with the backing and batting. You may use a sharp medium-lead or silver pencil on light background fabrics. Test the pencil marks to guarantee that they will wash out of your quilt top when quilting is complete; or be sure your quilting stitches cover the pencil marks. Mechanical pencils with very fine points may be used successfully to mark quilts.

Manufactured quilt-design templates are available in many designs and sizes and are cut out of a durable plastic template material which is easy to use.

To make a permanent quilt-design template, choose a template material on which to transfer the design. See-through plastic is the best as it will let you place the design while allowing you to see where it is in relation to your quilt design without moving it. Place the design on the quilt top where you want it and trace around it with your marking tool. Pick up the quilting template and place again; repeat marking.

No matter what marking method you use, remember—the marked lines should *never show* on the finished quilt. When the top is marked, it is ready for layering.

Preparing the Quilt Backing. The quilt backing is a very important feature of your quilt. In most cases, the materials list for each quilt in this book gives the size requirements for the backing, not the yardage needed. Exceptions to this are when the backing fabric is also used on the quilt top and yardage is given for that fabric.

A backing is generally cut at least 4" larger than the quilt top or 2" larger on all sides. For a 64" x 78" finished quilt, the backing would need to be at least 68" x 82".

To avoid having the seam across the center of the quilt backing, cut or tear one of the right-length pieces in half and sew half to each side of the second piece as shown in Figure 11.

Quilts that need a backing more than 88" wide may be pieced in horizontal pieces as shown in Figure 12.

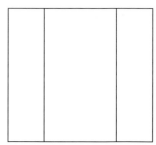

Figure 11
Center 1 backing piece with a piece on each side.

Figure 12
Horizontal seams may be used on backing pieces.

Layering the Quilt Sandwich.
Layering the quilt top with the batting and backing is time-consuming. Open the batting several days before you need it and place over a bed or flat on the floor to help flatten the creases caused from its being folded up in the bag for so long.

Iron the backing piece, folding in half both vertically and horizontally and pressing to mark centers.

If you will not be quilting on a frame, place the backing right side down on a clean floor or table. Start in the center and push any wrinkles or bunches flat. Use masking tape to tape the edges to the floor or large clips to hold the backing to the edges of the table. The backing should be taut.

Place the batting on top of the backing, matching centers using fold lines as guides; flatten out any wrinkles. Trim the batting to the same size as the backing.

Fold the quilt top in half lengthwise and place on top of the batting, wrong side against the batting, matching centers. Unfold quilt and, working from the center to the outside edges, smooth out any wrinkles or lumps.

To hold the quilt layers together for quilting, baste by hand or use safety pins. If basting by hand, thread a long thin needle with a long piece of unknotted white or off-white thread. Starting in the center and

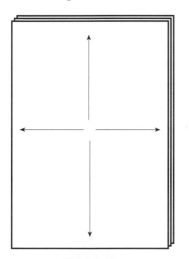

Figure 13
Baste from the center to the outside edges.

leaving a long tail, make 4"–6" stitches toward the outside edge of the quilt top, smoothing as you baste. Start at the center again and work toward the outside as shown in Figure 13.

If quilting by machine, you may prefer to use safety pins for holding your fabric sandwich together. Start in the center of the quilt and pin to the outside, leaving pins open until all are placed.

When you are satisfied that all layers are smooth, close the pins.

QUILTING

Hand Quilting. Hand quilting is the process of placing stitches through the quilt top, batting and backing to hold them together. While it is a functional process, it also adds beauty and loft to the finished quilt.

To begin, thread a sharp between needle with an 18" piece of quilting thread. Tie a small knot in the end of the thread. Position the needle about 1/2" to 1" away from the starting point on quilt top. Sink the needle through the top into the batting layer but not through the backing. Pull the needle up at the starting point of the quilting design. Pull the needle and thread until the knot sinks through the top into the batting (Figure 14).

Some stitchers like to take a backstitch here at the beginning while others prefer to begin the first stitch here. Take small, even running stitches along the marked quilting line (Figure 15). Keep one hand positioned underneath to feel the needle go all the way through to the backing.

Figure 14
Start the needle through the top layer of fabric 1/2"–1" away from quilting line with knot on top of fabric.

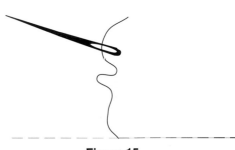

Figure 15
Make small, even running stitches on marked quilting line.

Machine Quilting. Successful machine quilting requires practice and a good relationship with your sewing machine.

TIPS & TECHNIQUES

Knots should not show on the quilt top or back. Learn to sink the knot into the batting at the beginning and ending of the quilting thread for successful stitches. Making 12–18 stitches per inch is a nice goal, but a more realistic goal is seven to nine stitches per inch. If you cannot accomplish this right away, strive for even stitches—all the same size—that look as good on the back as on the front.

When you have nearly run out of thread, wind the thread around the needle several times to make a small knot and pull it close to the

fabric. Insert the needle into the fabric on the quilting line and come out with the needle 1/2" to 1" away, pulling the knot into the fabric layers the same as when you started. Pull and cut thread close to fabric. The end should disappear inside after cutting. Some quilters prefer to take a backstitch with a loop through it for a knot to end.

You will perfect your quilting stitches as you gain experience, your stitches will get better with each project and your style will be uniquely your own.

Prepare the quilt for machine quilting in the same way as for hand quilting. Use safety pins to hold the layers together instead of basting with thread.

Presser-foot quilting is best used for straight-line quilting because the presser bar lever does not need to be continually lifted.

Set the machine on a longer stitch length (three or eight to 10 stitches to the inch). Too tight a stitch causes puckering and fabric tucks, either on the quilt top or backing. An even-feed or walking foot helps to eliminate the tucks and puckering by feeding the upper and lower layers through the machine evenly. Before you begin, loosen the amount of pressure on the presser foot.

Special machine-quilting needles work best to penetrate the three layers in your quilt.

Decide on a design. Quilting in the ditch is not quite as visible, but if you quilt with the feed dogs engaged, it means turning the quilt frequently. It is not easy to fit a rolled-up quilt through the small opening on the sewing machine head.

Meander quilting is the easiest way to machine-quilt—and it is fun. Meander quilting is done using an appliqué or darning foot with the feed dogs dropped. It is sort of like scribbling. Simply move the quilt top around under the foot and make stitches in a random pattern to fill the space. The same method may be used to outline a quilt design. The trick is the same as in hand-quilting; you are striving for stitches of uniform size. Your hands are in complete control of the design.

If machine-quilting is of interest to you, there are several very good books available at quilt shops that will help you become a successful machine quilter.

Tied Quilts, or Comforters. Would you rather tie your quilt layers together than quilt them? Tied quilts are often referred to as comforters. The advantage of tying is that it takes

so much less time and the required skills can be learned quickly.

If a top will be tied, choose a thick, bonded batting—one that will not separate during washing. For tying, use pearl cotton, embroidery floss, or strong yarn in colors that match or coordinate with the fabrics in your quilt top.

Decide on a pattern for tying. Many quilts are tied at the corners and centers of the blocks and at sashing joints. Try to tie every 4"–6". Special designs can be used for tying, but most quilts are tied in conventional ways. Begin tying in the center and work to the outside edges.

To make the tie, thread a large needle with a long thread (yarn, floss or crochet cotton); do not knot. Push the needle through the quilt top to the back, leaving a 3"–4" length on top. Move the needle to the next position without cutting thread. Take another stitch through the layers; repeat until thread is almost used up.

Cut thread between stitches, leaving an equal amount of thread on each stitch. Tie a knot with the two thread ends. Tie again to make a square knot referring to Figure 16. Trim thread ends to desired length.

Figure 16
Make a square knot as shown.

Finishing the Edges

After your quilt is tied or quilted, the edges need to be finished. Decide how you want the edges of your quilt finished before layering the backing and batting with the quilt top.

Without Binding—Self-Finish. There is one way to eliminate

adding an edge finish. This is done before quilting. Place the batting on a flat surface. Place the pieced top right side up on the batting. Place the backing right sides together with the pieced top. Pin and/or baste the layers together to hold flat referring to page 171.

Begin stitching in the center of one side using a 1/4" seam allowance, reversing at the beginning and end of the seam. Continue stitching all around and back to the beginning side. Leave a 12" or larger opening. Clip corners to reduce excess. Turn right side out through the opening. Slipstitch the opening closed by hand. The quilt may now be quilted by hand or machine.

The disadvantage to this method is that once the edges are sewn in, any creases or wrinkles that might form during the quilting process cannot be flattened out. Tying is the preferred method for finishing a quilt constructed using this method.

Bringing the backing fabric to the front is another way to finish the quilt's edge without binding. To accomplish this, complete the quilt as for hand or machine quilting. Trim the batting *only* even with the front. Trim the backing 1" larger than the completed top all around.

Turn the backing edge in 1/2" and then turn over to the front along edge of batting. The folded edge may be machine-stitched close to the edge through all layers, or blind-stitched in place to finish.

The front may be turned to the back. If using this method, a wider front border is needed. The backing and batting are trimmed 1" *smaller* than the top and the top edge is turned under 1/2" and then turned to the back and stitched in place.

One more method of self-finish may be used. The top and backing may be stitched together by hand at the edge. To accomplish this, all quilting must be stopped 1/2" from the quilt-top edge. The top and backing of the quilt are trimmed even and the batting is trimmed to 1/4"–1/2" smaller. The edges of the top and backing are turned in 1/4"–1/2" and blind-stitched together at the very edge.

These methods do not require the use of extra fabric and save time in preparation of binding strips; they are not as durable as an added binding.

Binding. The technique of adding extra fabric at the edges of the quilt is called binding. The binding encloses the edges and adds an extra layer of fabric for durability.

To prepare the quilt for the addition of the binding, trim the batting and backing layers flush with the top of the quilt using a rotary cutter and ruler or shears. Using a walking-foot attachment (sometimes called an even-feed foot attachment), machine-baste the three layers together all around approximately 1/8" from the cut edge.

The list of materials given with each quilt in this book often includes a number of yards of self-made or purchased binding. Bias binding may be purchased in packages and in many colors. The advantage to self-made binding is that you can use fabrics from your quilt to coordinate colors.

Double-fold, straight-grain binding and double-fold, bias-grain binding are two of the most commonly used types of binding.

Double-fold, straight-grain binding is used on smaller projects with right-angle corners. Double-fold, bias-grain binding is best suited for bed-size quilts or quilts with rounded corners.

To make double-fold, straight-grain binding, cut 2"-wide strips of fabric across the width or down the length of the fabric totaling the perimeter of the quilt plus 10". The strips are joined as shown in Figure 17 and pressed in half wrong sides together along the length using an iron on a cotton setting with *no* steam.

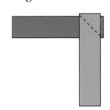

Figure 17
Join binding strips in a diagonal seam to eliminate bulk as shown.

Lining up the raw edges, place the binding on the top of the quilt and begin sewing (again using the walking foot) approximately 6" from the beginning of the binding strip. Stop sewing 1/4" from the first corner, leave the needle in the quilt, turn and sew diagonally to the corner as shown in Figure 18.

Figure 18
Sew to within 1/4" of corner; leave needle in quilt, turn and stitch diagonally off the corner of the quilt.

Fold the binding at a 45-degree angle up and away from the quilt as shown in Figure 19 and back down flush with the raw edges. Starting at the top raw edge of the quilt, begin sewing the next side as shown in Figure 20. Repeat at the next three corners.

Figure 19
Fold binding at a 45-degree angle up and away from quilt as shown.

Figure 20
Fold the binding strips back down, flush with the raw edge, and begin sewing.

As you approach the beginning of the binding strip, stop stitching and overlap the binding 1/2" from the edge, trim. Join the two ends with a 1/4" seam allowance and press the seam open. Reposition the joined binding along the edge of the quilt and resume stitching to the beginning.

To finish, bring the folded edge of the binding over the raw edges and blind-stitch the binding in place over the machine-stitching line on the backside. Hand-miter the corners on the back as shown in Figure 21.

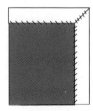

Figure 21
Miter and stitch the corners as shown.

If you are making a quilt to be used on a bed, you will want to use double-fold, bias-grain bindings because the many threads that cross each other along the fold at the edge of the quilt make it a more durable binding.

Cut 2"-wide bias strips from a large square of fabric. Join the strips as illustrated in Figure 17 and press the seams open. Fold the beginning end of the bias strip 1/4" from the raw edge and press. Fold the joined strips in half along the long side, wrong sides together, and press with *no* steam (Figure 22).

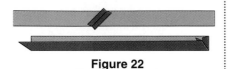

Figure 22
Fold end in and
press strip in half.

Follow the same procedures as previously described for preparing the quilt top and sewing the binding to the quilt top. Treat the corners just as you treated them with straight-grain binding.

Since you are using bias-grain binding, you do have the option to just eliminate the corners if this option doesn't interfere with the patchwork in the quilt. Round the corners off by placing one of your dinner plates at the corner and rotary-cutting the gentle curve (Figure 23).

Figure 23
Round corners to eliminate
square-corner finishes.

As you approach the beginning of the binding strip, stop stitching and lay the end across the beginning so it will slip inside the fold. Cut the end at a 45-degree angle so the raw edges are contained inside the beginning of the strip (Figure 24).

Resume stitching to the beginning. Bring the fold to the back of the quilt and hand-stitch as previously described.

Figure 24
End the binding strips as shown.

Overlapped corners are not quite as easy as rounded ones, but a bit easier than mitering. To make over-lapped corners, sew binding strips to opposite sides of the quilt top. Stitch edges down to finish. Trim ends even.

Sew a strip to each remaining side, leaving 1 1/2"–2" excess at each end. Turn quilt over and fold binding down even with previous finished edge as shown in Figure 25.

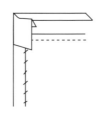

Figure 25
Fold end of binding even with
previous edge.

Fold binding in toward quilt and stitch down as before, enclosing the previous bound edge in the seam as shown in Figure 26. It may be necessary to trim the folded-down section to reduce bulk.

Figure 26
An overlapped corner is not quite as
neat as a mitered corner.

MAKING CONTINUOUS BIAS BINDING

Instead of cutting individual bias strips and sewing them together, you may make continuous bias binding.

Cut a square 18" x 18" from chosen binding fabric. Cut the square once on the diagonal to make two

triangles as shown in Figure 27. With right sides together, sew the two triangles together with a 1/4" seam allowance as shown in Figure 28; press seam open to reduce bulk.

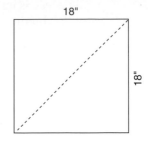

Figure 27
Cut 18" square on the diagonal.

Figure 28
Sew the triangles together.

Mark lines every 2 1/4" on the wrong side of the fabric as shown in Figure 29. Bring the short ends together, right sides together, offsetting one line as shown in Figure 30 to make a tube; stitch. This will seem awkward.

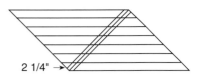

Figure 29
Mark lines every 2 1/4".

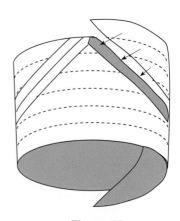

Figure 30
Sew short ends together,
offsetting lines to make a tube.

Begin cutting at point A as shown in Figure 31; continue cutting along marked line to make one continuous strip. Fold strip in half along length with wrong sides together; press. Sew to quilt edges as instructed previously for bias binding.

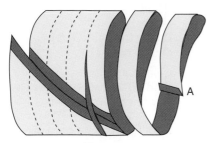

Figure 31
Cut along marked lines, starting at A.

FINAL TOUCHES

If your quilt will be hung on the wall, a hanging sleeve is required. Other options include purchased plastic rings or fabric tabs. The best choice is a fabric sleeve, which will evenly distribute the weight of the

quilt across the top edge, rather than at selected spots where tabs or rings are stitched, keep the quilt hanging straight and not damage the batting.

To make a sleeve, measure across the top of the finished quilt. Cut an 8"-wide piece of muslin equal to that length—you may need to seam several muslin strips together to make the required length.

Fold in 1/4" on each end of the muslin strip and press. Fold again and stitch to hold. Fold the muslin strip lengthwise with right sides together.

Sew along the long side to make a tube. Turn the tube right side out; press with seam at bottom or centered on the back.

Hand-stitch the tube along the top of the quilt and the bottom of the tube to the quilt back making sure the quilt lies flat. Stitches should not go through to the front of the quilt and don't need to be too close together as shown in Figure 32.

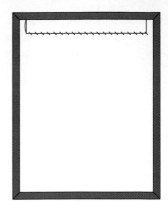

Figure 32
Sew a sleeve to the top back of the quilt.

Slip a wooden dowel or long curtain rod through the sleeve to hang.

When the quilt is finally complete, it should be signed and dated. Use a permanent pen on the back of the quilt. Other methods include cross-stitching your name and date on the front or back or making a permanent label which may be stitched to the back.

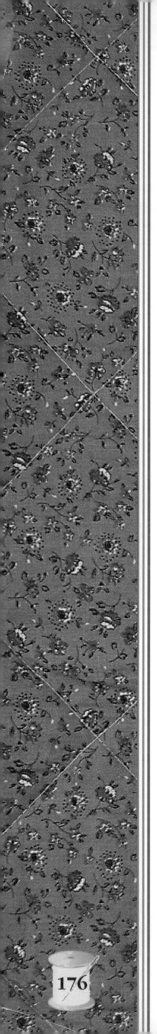

Special Thanks

We would like to thank the talented quilt designers whose work is featured in this collection.

Fabrics & Supplies

Page 8: Four-Patch Tie—Butterick pattern #6663

Page 8: Four-Patch Vest—Mission Valley Textiles plaid fabrics

Page 11: Double Four-Patch Vest—New Home Sewing Machine Company Memory Craft 9000 sewing machine, Fairfield Soft Touch cotton batting

Page 25: Patriotic Denim Shirt—Pellon Wonder-Under fusible transfer web and Stitch-n-Tear fabric stabilizer

Page 42: Quick Quilter's Vest—Simplicity pattern #8744

Page 57: Stained-Glass Window—New Home Sewing Machine Company Memory Craft 9000 sewing machine

Page 70: Patchwork Ornaments—Coats & Clark gold cording

Page 74: Golden Elegance—New Home Sewing Machine Company Memory Craft 9000 sewing machine, Prizm gold hologram thread from GlissenGloss, Fairfield Soft Touch cotton batting

Page 82: Poinsettia Christmas—Heat 'n Bond Lite fusible transfer web from Therm O Web, Madiera rayon machine-embroidery thread

Page 88: Folded Pinwheel Quilt—Moda Fabrics, Hobbs Heirloom Premium cotton batting, Sew/Fit Add-A-Table sewing machine extension table

Page 98: Buckeye Beauty—Benartex fabrics, Mountain Mist batting, Sew/Fit Snap-Shot Ruler

Page 118: Sunny Lanes—Master Piece 45 ruler and Static Stickers

Page 143: Double Four-Patch—Fairfield Soft Touch cotton batting, machine-quilted by Dianne Hodgkins.

Page 150: Midnight Stars—Master Piece 45 ruler and Static Stickers

Page 153: Broken Dishes—Fairfield Soft Touch cotton batting, machine-quilted by Dianne Hodgkins.

Page 160: Chutes & Ladders—Master Piece 45 ruler and Static Stickers